WHAT PEOPLE AR

SAS

This is absolutely freakin' brilliant and every ...
every woman, but every man too, must read this.
It'll inspire you to do great things from the first word. This book is
electric and Lisa Clark is on fire.
Barefoot Doctor, Bestselling Author

SASSY is a fabtabulously sexy self-help book which will help you find
your own super-hero girl power within!
It oozes wisdom, humour and inspiration. From great tips on how
to date yourself, to knowing your own fabulosity and trusting
yourself, this is a guide-book for all modern day goddesses who want
to live life large by being themselves.
Suzy Greaves, author of *Making The Big Leap*

I love *SASSY* and its 'shaking her tail feather' Goddess author, Lisa
Clark – we need more of this kind of supportive sisterhood ! She's a
kindred spirit alright, she loves the beach (was possibly a mermaid in
a former life) and gives us sassy tips to make the most of our Spiritual,
Authentic, Sensual & Sensational selves!
There's some great tips from simple ways to connect with spirituality through learning about Moon cycles (and taking a moon bath)
and reminding yourself what makes you happy. It's an inspirational
fun read to help you get back in balance and be your very own sassy
self. I've signed up to being Sassy – will you?
Janey Lee Grace, author of *Look Great Naturally without ditching the
lipstick* and runs www.imperfectlynatural.com

This book will not only make you grin from ear to ear, but it will
motivate and support you in becoming a fearless, feisty female! Learn
to love yourself and create the life of your dreams with the help of
super sassy lady, Lisa Clark – you'll be glad you did.
Katy Evans, Editor of Soul&Spirit magazine

Lisa's lyrical, magical-sprinkled words light up the page with such
gusto you feel ready to start actively setting about achieving your
goals. It's like having that most marvelous of friend who is cheering
you on all the way – with a side order of SASS, of course! Lisa is one
of those amazing women who really wants to empower girl-kind and
see you reach that potential, in fact, she insists on it.
Stephanie Brookes, author of *How to be a Spiritual Goddess: Bring a
Little Cosmic Magic into Your Life*

I completely fell in love with Lisa's concept of SASSYology and all it
stands for. She supports other women in a non patronising and fun

loving way – shining a pink spotlight on you and urging you to indulge in what you love and to love yourself without feeling guilty about it. Written in a simplistic, candid yet inspirational tone, Lisa's words are motivional and peppered with humour and original phrases that Ive come to use and live by.

I love the tip about looking at your life as a play list and if that play list is crap in places, delete a few tracks and design one you adore! But unlike other self help style books, this one gives you a guided tour of how to achieve it and makes you feel like Lisa is your best friend waving a bright pink flag and rolling out the pink carpet for you toward Destination Awesome.

Bethanie Lunn, author of *Modern Girl's Guide to Fabulousness*

What a book! So much vibrant energy oozes from every page that it's like having your very own pom pom wielding cheerleader. This is the book if you want to open yourself up, to all you can be, in a fun vivacious, sensual way.

Lisa writes naturally with laugh out loud humour and is so honest you'll think you know her. Which you will. Chutzpah is an understatement.

Read this, get your sass on.

Barbara Ford Hammond, author of *The Psychic Way: Fine-tuning Your Intuition*

Lisa Clark is a magical writer with attitude. She struts her stuff because she knows it! *SASSY* is the perfect adjective for a woman whose writing beams energy, wit and knowledge.

Mary Bryce, It's Fate magazine

Lisa Clark is a shining magenta magnaplasm of incandescent light. Her words will strike deep into your heart and activate a world of what you already know is true: You are SASSY. You are a Goddess. You are capable and aglow and your very own superhero. A must read for every woman!

Goddess Leonie Dawson, Creator of www.GoddessGuidebook.com

THIS is the book I've been waiting for. It's as if Lisa Clark has sat me down and told me everything I need to know about living life to its very fullest.

THEN, she's called in her most inspiring friends too. It's sort of a lifestyle intervention. It's honest, open and funny and it's practical too. The advice and tools are there so that each reader can take out what they need and like me, will know that THEY have to do the work. Except that the work seems mostly fun and that's what's really good about it. It's a guide to living, working and being totally authentic and really, truly happy in every way. I feel like *SASSY* was written just for me but I suspect that everyone else might feel that way!

Lyndsey Whiteside, Owner, Inspired PR

SASSY

The go-for-it girl's guide to
becoming mistress of your destiny

SASSY

The go-for-it girl's guide to
becoming mistress of your destiny

Lisa Clark

SASSY BOOKS

Winchester, UK
Washington, USA

First published by Sassy Books, 2012
Sassy Books is an imprint of John Hunt Publishing Ltd., Laurel House, Station Approach,
Alresford, Hants, SO24 9JH, UK
office1@jhpbooks.net
www.johnhuntpublishing.com
www.sassy-books.com

For distributor details and how to order please visit the 'Ordering' section on our website.

Text copyright: Lisa Clark 2011

ISBN: 978 1 84694 520 5

A CIP catalogue record for this book is available from the British Library.

Design: Stuart Davies

Printed and bound by CPI Group (UK) Ltd, Croydon, CR0 4YY

We operate a distinctive and ethical publishing philosophy in all
areas of our business, from our global network of authors to
production and worldwide distribution.

CONTENTS

Acknowledgements

The biggest love and hot-pink lipstick kisses to…

Miss Aimee Louise Richards – I have a gazillion things to thank you for; eating chocolate buttons with me, singing random songs down the phone, dee-licious life-changing trips to Paris, but right now, the most important thing, is to thank you for being you. I heart you Miss Aimz.

Susie Rains – I know that *'its all part of the process'* has been our catchphrase for a few years now, but it was. And now we're reaping the delicious rewards. You were right, you're ALWAYS right, and I am SO lucky to have you as my best friend.

Jason Hood – for being my teacher o' Reiki, fellow drinker o' pink fizz and the most beautiful, beautiful friend – I love you, mister.

Donna & Wendy Carter – I love that I get to call you two beautiful, talented and incredible women my friends, even if you do make me say words that would make a sailor blush – mwwwooooaaahhh!

Brett Gardner – boy o' wonder, thanks for being awesome. Always. Love you..

Diane Evans – thanks so much for sharing your story, and for being my gal pal o' fabulosity – big, big love.

John and Cheryl – I don't even have the words to thank you for everything you've both done for me in the past few years. I love you both.

The gorgeous Anisa Topan for sending me pictures o' glittery pugs and hooking me up with the dee-licious Sam Roddick – high fives, g-friend!

Team SASSY - Lyndsey, girl o' PR wonder and Jules, web mistress supreme-o – you both rock hard.

The Daring Dames – my absolute inspir-o-girls. I can't believe you all agreed to come play in my world o' SASSY, I am in awe of the magick you sprinkle on the world – Immodesty, Kelliana, Sam, Sarah, Star, Francesca, Kitty, Leonie and Darcy – thank you for sharing your talent and complete gorgeousness – mwwwoooah!

My beautiful, big-hearted, husband-to-be, my hot viking beau, Rich – you are absolute proof that dreams come true, miracles *do* happen and that life is infinitely sweeter when shared with someone you love. And I do love you. More than chocolate. There, I said it. Thank you for reigniting my spark for life, for sharing sunsets and sunrises with me, for waking me up to moon-bathe in the light of the full moon, for inspiring me, for gifting me a writer-girl room, for believing in me, and for being you. Beautiful, big-hearted you. I thank every single star that we exist on the same celestial plain.

Foreword

Immodesty Blaize

SASSY is a girl's uplifting companion, a glittering, diamond encrusted key to unlocking your inner Super-Hero-Girl. Barbie take a hike…and pompous self-help gurus take note; because this is delightfully candid, smart, supportive and – well, sassy.

'Live the dream' is the buzz phrase du jour, as though just thinking it will somehow magically make our fairy tale lives appear from nowhere. But straight-talking SASSY asks you questions, and gives you the tools to get what you want for yourself, to be supercharged with self-knowledge, on your terms.

I thought I'd heard just about every inspirational quote under the sun, especially having a job that doesn't allow for paper-bag-over-the-head kinds of days. Thank god then for this book, something fresh, breezy and practical. This lady talks sense, a lot of her advice I identified with personally from my own journey to gaining the confidence needed to allow me to fulfil what many consider to be an unconventional career on stage. SASSY will be for many girls like a little firework of a bedside bible bestowed by a kookily fabulous fairygodsister who makes it all sound so obvious…because really, it is – life is for living, not a ratrace, and anyone can blow away the self doubt demons and unlock their inner Super-Hero-Girl…especially with the support of SASSY. Make the world your fabulous oyster, enjoy!

Love, Immodesty x

This book is dedicated to my beautiful goddess-daughter, Ella Louise Rogers. Always be a first rate version of you, gorgeous girl, not a second rate version of someone else, you're far too special for that.
I love you x

Introduction

What is SASSY?
SASSY is the **S**piritual, **A**uthentic, **S**ensual & **S**ensational **Y**ou. When all five elements combine, it unleashes the innate awesomeness of the most kick-ass members o' lady-kind who came before us. SASSY is your magickal chutzpah, your go-for-it girl juice, your cosmic ju-ju, your very own super-girl super-power.

Woah! So I get super-powers?
As any super-hero-girl will testify, fully embracing your epic super-hero-girl powers takes time. But yep, you do. In fact, shall I let you into a little secret? You've already got them. They're just lying dormant, deep down inside of you. Your job is to discover them, learn about them, work them out, and really get to grips with them before you can truly own them and use them for good. Just ask Wonder Woman. She was rubbish with a lasso when she started out.

But the good news is, it's not difficult, far from it. How do I know? Because if it were, I *certainly* wouldn't be doing it, and I, gorgeous girls, am *totally* in my SASSY power. Nope, all you've got to do is be ready.

Why? Because your life will change in a gazillion different ways and well... you really *do* have to be ready for that.

How do I get me some o' that SASSY power?
Sorcery.

Now, this particular kind o' sorcery, the SASSY kind, isn't all puffs of smoke and eye-of-newt like in the *Harry Potter* movies, nor is it tie-dye, lentils and hours upon hours of deep meditation. Nope, SASSY sorcery is a very special glitter-sprinkled blend of the very best kind of magick, it's feel-good magick. It doesn't mean that it's all pink and fluff-filled, I mean, yes, there is definitely some pink involved, and I make no apologies for that, but believe me, when used properly, with purpose and intent, this stuff is crazy-powerful. SASSY sorcery will allow you to splash in your very own bubble bath of fabulousness and will bestow upon you every super-hero-girl power you'll ever need to conjure up happy moods, change the way you see yourself when you look in the mirror, positively radiate confidence, own any room you walk into, improve every aspect of your life - health, career, relationships, finances - and most importantly, find your very own SASSY, the magick that's deep, deep inside you.

When you practice SASSY Sorcery, as in *really* practice it, something amazing happens. Think Elizabeth Taylor playing the ultimate seductress, *Cleopatra*. Hot, right? Well multiply that by 1000 then you might begin to get the idea. You'll become quite possibly the most bewitching bombshell. The kind o' gal who is so completely in tune with her powers that you can identify, go after, and most importantly, conjure up and invoke whatever it is you want in life, all while dancing to your very own beat and wearing completely inappropriate footwear. And like I said earlier, you *really* have to be ready for that, because not only will you walk taller, you'll have an 'I had *amazing* sex last night' smile on your face a LOT of the time and people will have an insta-attraction to you without entirely knowing why – it's just how you'll roll.

I discovered the full power of SASSY Sorcery while on a girly weekend in the land of Oh la la, Paris. It was 2008 and my gorgeous gal-pal, Aimee and I had run away. Well, for the New Year at least. We had both cut ties with our boyfriends at the time, so we thought what better way for two rather fabulous, newly single girls to see the New Year in, than under the gorgeous sparkles of the Eiffel Tower? So we did. We maxed out our credit cards, we stayed in a gorgeous hotel, we watched beautiful ladies dance topless at the *Crazy Horse*, we ate delicious macaroons à la

Carrie Bradshaw and Marie Antoinette before her and it was there, in beautiful, delightfully divine Paris, that I performed my first act of SASSY Sorcery, except I didn't know that's what it was back then. I want to tell you all about it right now, but hey, you'll find out soon enough. All you need to know is that, at that moment, the planets aligned, they did a little cosmic wiggle and the beautiful tower o' light blew me a kiss to seal the deal, because what happened after that day... Wow. Now that really has been magick.

Before we start, you need to know that I'm not a guru, although I do have a rather cute li'l Buddha belly that I rub for magickal insight. I'm not a philosopher either, although I do quite fancy myself as one, and, if I say so myself, I do look rather hot in an all-black ensemble. Nope, I'm just a girl who believes in the power o' SASSY. I grew up on a council estate and never quite fitted the cookie-cutter version of how a girl *should* look, act and be. At school, as anyone who ever went to a comprehensive school will tell you, not fitting in truly sucked. In my world of SASSY however, not fitting society's so-called 'norm' is positively encouraged. You see, even when I was dying my hair a variety of crazy colours, rimming my eyes with black kohl and writing the name of my latest boy crush on my school exercise books, I always thought that, despite the huge curveballs life kept throwing my way, there *had* to be something else. I desperately wanted something to believe in, so I believed in fairy-tales, I believed in happy ever-afters because there simply had to be something more fabulous in store for me, something that was truly magickal. Looking back, I'm guessing that was the divine/goddess/spiritual homegirl/source/all that is/universe – delete as applicable – giving me a friendly manicured-finger poke, delicately whispering in my ear that I was right, there really was a whole world of magick, insights and adventure for me to go and explore.

So that's what I did. The girl that believed in magick, became a kick-ass SASSYologist. What is a SASSYologist? Simply put, she's a wise woman, who uses her innate superpowers, to conjure, enchant and bewitch her way to a life of complete awesomeness. She salutes the wild women and goddess-girls of the past: Boudicca, Joan of Arc, Marilyn Monroe, Cleopatra, Hekate, Isis, Gypsy Rose Lee, while seeking new ways to blaze a sparkly pink trail of glitter and sparkles on her own SASSY path.

So what do you think?

Are you ready to rock and rule at this thing they call life? Want to do it in a wiggle dress and feather boa? Or biker boots and a vest? Whatever your chosen attire, this book will help you do that. As a life coach, I've worked with so many fabulous women in my Sassy Sessions who desperately wanted me to spill, to share my secret weapons o' SASSY, so I have. This book has come directly from my first hand experience of discovering my own SASSY super powers and harnessing them, Boudicca-style, to become a life-creatrix, mistress of my own destiny. I'm also beside myself with excitement because some of my very own idol-girls, ladies that completely rock my world, have come to strut their very own SASSY and share their insight, wisdom and magickal powers with you too, make sure you look out for my Daring Dames – they're truly, truly kick-ass. It's raw, from-the-heart stuff for anyone who needs proof that magick *does* exist and a permission slip to dream the most juice-filled delicious dreams and then go right ahead and make them happen.

Oh, I don't want to tell you how to read a book, but to experience it fully, I absolutely, positively encourage you to not *just* read it, but to write notes in the margins, dance with it, share the bits you love with friends, give it a smooch, sleep with it under your pillow – most importantly, participate.

I dare you.

Big, beautiful heart-filled love stuff,

Lisa x

The SASSYologist

The SASSY-festo

Just so you know, as controversial as this may sound, I really struggle with the 'f' word. I don't know if it's the negative connotations and stereotypes that have come with it over the years – bra burning (I would NEVER burn a bra, those bad boys are freakin' expensive and far too pretty), man-hating (I HEART men A LOT) and the whole un-feminine thing (I REALLY love heels) but whatever it is, rightly or wrongly, the term 'feminist' just doesn't sit right with me. It might just be that I don't really like labels in general, I especially dislike the ones found in dresses, mainly because so many women feel the need to measure their self-worth based on the number they find on it. In fact, the only label I'll ever be willing to accept is that I'm SASSY.

An always-learning, always creating, woman of awesome.

A feisty, emotive, love-hard woman in my total power who has amazing sex, has fears and insecurities but meets them head on, crushes on my own reflection in the mirror, is honest and real – which means sometimes, I'll mess up, oh, and is able to wear MAC make-up rather fabulously, obv.

Now, another thing you need to know about me is that I'm often accused of being a bit 'fluffy'. And that's cool, because, do you know what? I am. And it's taken me a while, but now I'm totally unapologetic for that. I have a penchant for boy bands, I meditate in a leopard print-slanket and tiara, I love pretty things, especially Vivienne Westwood shoes, I paint my nails every evening and I totally heart the colour pink. But, I'm also a kick-ass businesswoman, a deeply spiritual thinker and well... I'm complex. I love to learn about the stars and the wonders of the universe AND I love to watch *E! Entertainment*, I fight tirelessly for the rights of girls and women to have all the information they need to make informed decisions about their lives AND I interview popstars and celebrities. I care passionately about the self-development of women AND I love kissing boys. I am a mass of fabulous contradictions.

Now, there's no hard-and-fast rules to actually being SASSY, it's totally YOU-nique to you, but just so you know, once your SASSY superpowers have been unleashed, it'll be really hard NOT to want to do all of the following, so why resist?

Don't diss on fellow members o' lady-kind – we need to love, support and nurture each other, NOT bitch, compete and draw red rings around each other's wobbly bits in trash mags.

Take responsibility for your own happiness and joy quota – It's up to you, and only you, with a little help from moi, obv., to awaken your SASSY superpowers, learn about them and then use them like a super-hero-girl to do seriously good super-hero-girl stuff in the world. Let's not blame boykind for absolutely everything, eh?

Be a tigress, seek pleasure – this life is way too short NOT to do the things you heart. When you know who, or what, makes your belly do front flips and your heart skip a beat, chase it, enjoy it, fully indulge in it, give thanks for it, and then lick your lips in complete satisfaction. Life is yummo.

Embrace your contradictions and most importantly, don't apologise for them – It's really okay to indulge in the work of Anais Nin *and* Jackie Collins. You can be feisty and fabulous *and* emo and fearful in equal measures. It's the beauty o' being you and you are a beauty, just so you know.

Go where there are no paths and make your own killer-heel-shaped footprints – I love nothing more than to read how a student with zilcho money can go on to make over £90,000 a year by blogging outfit ensembles, but if no one has done what you want to do, don't let that stop you. Trail blaze – you can do it, use your superpowers!

Talk about ALL aspects of being a girl in this world - and that involves dropping our li'l miss perfection masks and having frank, deep and open conversations about messing up, being afraid, sex, masturbation, orgasms, passions and fantasies too – go there, g-friend – I dare you!

Embrace all the things that make you completely YOU-nique – because seriously, fitting in is really rather boring. Embrace and totally love-up all your crazy habits and collections, your penchant for watching NCIS (admit it, LL Cool J's dimples are hot, non?) your work, your relationship, your slightly out-there vocab, the spiritual practices you dig – being SASSY is about being YOU. Without the fear of ridicule, because as Dita Von Teese once said, *'only mediocrity is free from ridicule – so dare to be different!'* High fives to that, Miss D!

It took me far too many years to actually *get* it. To *not* want to fit in with the popular girls, to *not* want to dress like fashion magazines dictated I should, to fly my SASSY freak flag high and embrace ALL the qualities that make me the most fabulous version of Lisa I can possibly be. I am Lisa, I LOVE being Lisa and quite frankly, I am really rather awesome at it.

Don't mind me, I'm just going to high five myself!

Now, while I'm assuming you're reading this with an open heart and mind, all I ask is that, no matter what, as you read, you absolutely go with your gut. Not only where the book is concerned, but with life too. I've got a Buddha belly – yep, it's round and a li'l chubby – but more than that, it's my inner guidance system, like a sat nav for the soul, it's what I rely on to let me know what works and what doesn't work for me, and it never, ever fails me. I sometimes ignore it, but when I do, life just goes... well, wrong. So, if what you read here feels right for you, then cool, go forth super-girl o' SASSY, and spread nothing but the good stuff throughout the cosmoverse, but the most important thing about being *really* SASSY is to find what works for YOU. Try things out; see how they fit for you. Does one particular method really speak to you? Question how it makes you feel. Throughout this book, what I'll be doing is sharing what works for me. *My* SASSY formula to unleashing *my* super powers o' SASSY and becoming mistress o' *my* destiny. Now, if I do say so myself, it's a pretty freakin' awesome one, but don't just take my word for it. Try it, feel it, work with it – then create your own SASSY-festo, write your own book of SASSY. This, and the books that follow, are simply a guide to help you discover, create and nurture awesomeness. Your life is *your* road trip, and so it's up to you what route you take, where you stop off, who you hang out with and what, and who you do en route, ok?

So, are you in?

The declaration o' SASSY

I, (insert your name here).., declare that I am absolutely ready to channel my inner Boudicca, take the reigns, and finally become mistress of my own amazing destiny – wooohhhoooo! I am woman, hear me roar, damn it!

Name:...

Date:..

Have you signed up? High fives, sweet thing! Your life is about to get seriously SASSY!

SPIRITUAL

"...Happiness cannot be travelled to, owned, earned, worn or consumed. Happiness is the spiritual experience of living every minute with love, grace and gratitude..."
Denis Waitley

So what do *you* think when you hear the term 'spirituality?'

Tie-dye wearing, incense burning hippy types? Or a totally zen-like, bendy-wendy guru in an Ashram in India? Spirituality is not an exclusive members-only club that you get to join when you chant 'om', meditate for 6 hours a day, wear floaty clothes and buy your over-priced ticket to a six-week retreat in an obscenely beautiful part of the world. If you feel called to do those things, do them, do them with a big love-filled heart, but also know that every day, in every way, you have insta-access to your own super-hero-girl power of spirituality. In fact, it doesn't matter whether you believe in God, magick, Goddesses, angels, the law of attraction or Jedi mind power, we've ALL got an Access All Areas pass to spirituality and a shopping trip, watching a sunrise, applying lipstick, eating a cupcake can be just as much, if not more of a spiritual experience than getting face time with the ever-so smiley, big-hearted Dalai Lama. (Although, if you ever get the chance to meet him, you really should, he seems like quite the dude.)

Spirituality is a kick-ass super power, it's my fail-safe trip to the happy stuff, and like all the SASSY powers you're about to discover, the good news is, it's all there, wrapped in a YOU-shaped package just waiting to be discovered. Spirituality is not religion, spirituality, to me, is when my actions and every day practices beat in sync with my big, beautiful heart. This literally flicks my SASSY switch to 'on' and I become a neon-pink flashing sign of awesome. Pretty much anything I do, or have done, that's authentic and meaningful and truly matters, is done when I hook up with the goddess, my spiritual homegirl. Some of my every day practices and ways that I connect, you'll read about in this chapter, and I urge you to give them a go, but I also insist that you dig deep inside o' yourself and feel that part of you that experiences serendipitous moments o' synchronicity, y'know that feeling? The one when you follow your gut and you're proven right? Feel it, and hold it tight. Now, and here's the fun bit, find out the ways to really tap into YOUR spirituality. To find the acts, the practices, and the actions that will beat in time with the beat of your own spiritual drum. It's when the really amazingly good stuff happens. Promise.

Maybe it's because I'm a Scorpio, (Scorpios are naturally drawn to all things esoteric), but I've never been able to follow just one particular spiritual practice, mostly because I'm far too fickle and there are so many delicious practices to try. I've studied reiki, Quaballah, crystals, astrology, runes, Wicca, Buddhism, Christianity, I've had my aura cleansed and my chakras re-aligned, I've met my spirit guides, had my palms read, been on shamanic journeys and tapped into Theta brainwaves to connect to Source, and that's just for starters.

Now, I've had a complete ball exploring these fabulous spirituality treats, I've had moments of total clarity, felt deep frustration and met the most interesting, crazy, bizarre and beautiful people, but you've got to be really careful not to over-eat at what the gorgeous Sara Beak, author of *The Red Book*, calls 'the spiritual buffet,' as too much esoteric candy can make a girl feel ever-so queasy.

If this is all feeling like a crazy amount of woo-woo right now, start by just taking a deep breath and simply choose to believe. Make a little pact with your sweet self, right here, right now, and simply ask for proof. A sign that you're on the right path to your awesome destiny, it may come from a lyric in a song, a word written on a passing van, a letter in the post, a change in situation, or an opportunity where before there wasn't one, just ask, believe, and when that sign arrives, I defy you not to do a little happy dance, okay?!

Self-belief

Okay, super-hero-girl-in-training, your mission, should you choose to accept it, (and you absolute should, btw.) is to lasso yourself a never-ending supply of self-belief. Why? Because it's a must-have if you want huge helpings of success, kick-assness and the happy stuff. When you have it, you feel on top of the world: calm, confident and good about yourself. You feel like you deserve the best and you attract good fortune like one of those Chinese kitties with the waving arm. Without it though, you lose all fuzzy feelings o' fabulousness. Boo. So, I guess you want to know how to work that lasso *Wonder Woman* style, right?

It works a little something like this: we only value ourselves as highly as we trust ourselves. Self-trust maintains our self-belief. So, what do you think? Do you trust yourself? Sometimes the trust tank can flicker between maximo trust – maybe you're super-confident in how you rock it in the workplace, to zilcho trust – but perhaps find it harder to do so in your personal relationships. You might have experienced a setback that's knocked your self-trust to pieces: illness, bereavement, separation or any change in your lifestyle can do this. Trust is a big deal; it involves a commitment to holding positive beliefs about the universe at a very deep level; it requires an intimate smooch-fest with your inner self. One way to help you develop this beautiful relationship is to learn to listen, and act on, your intuition.

Listening to your intuition

Can you trust your intuition? Do you know where to look for it? You know you're tapping into your intuition when you have a 'hunch' about something, when you know something to be true even if you haven't been told about it, you just *know*. My intuition sits deep in my Buddha belly, and if I ask a question of it, I gently rub my solar plexus, my personal power chakra, and wait for it to respond, which it always does, along with a whisper in my ear. If the situ is good, then I will feel butterflies of enthusiasm and anticipation, if it's not right, it feels like a dull ache, an uncomfy, not-nice feeling. This is just how it is for me; you'll need to find out for yourself what your intuitive feelings are and what they mean to you.

Sit quietly in a comfy place and take some deep yoga-like breathes. Relax your body and your mind. Focus your thoughts on your intuition.

What feelings do you associate with your intuition?

....

....

....

Are these feelings welcome or fearful?

....

....

....

Think of three times that you have followed your intuition and things turned out well.

....

....

....

Write down three things that your intuition has been urging you to do. These might only be small things, like, write a letter, read a specific book, or they might be about bigger things like moving house or ending that relationship.

....

....

....

Why have you not acted on the advice of your intuition?

....

....

....

Your intuition gives you important information and will speak to you through urges, feelings and flashes of insight. The more you use it, the more juicy goodness it will give you. To really hear your intuition, you need to listen to your inner thoughts and feelings.

Your intuition will always draw you to things that give you energy and encourage your creativity. Perhaps you have a great desire to change your life in some way but keep creating excuses that stop you putting your plans into action. Maybe you're afraid to follow your intuition because it involves change and risk taking. You can never trust yourself if you're denying the voice of your intuition: your levels of self-belief and self-respect will be low and so you will find it hard to trust the rest of the universe.

If it's to be, it's up to me

Anyone that knows me will tell you, before I became a super-hero-girl o' SASSY, I was the world's worst decision maker. It really was all I could do to decide what knickers to wear in the morning, (I need to get myself a set of those *days of the week* knickers, that would at least make *that* decision easier!). So when it comes to the big decisions – life, love and everything in between – I wanted to go hide under the duvet with an industrial sized bar of chocolate, indefinitely.

But when you're SASSY, that's simply not an option.

You have to take responsibility for your actions, and while you can, and should, accept advice and guidance from, mentors, friends and family, ultimately, the nitty-gritty, down-and-dirty decision making about you, your path, your thoughts and actions, is down to one person.

You.

It also doesn't help if you're fickle. Which, FYI, I absolutely was. Fickleness leads to indecisiveness. Indecisiveness leads to no decision at all. No decision leads to lack o' life. Lack o' life = big pile of waste, regret and not-niceness.

Which is why, when you find yourself in a fug of fickleness and indecisiveness, your intuition is your ultimate go-to tool, but be sure to listen really carefully, because unless dealt with properly, the Funkatron (you'll find out more about the Funkatron later in the book – be ready to boo and hiss, it's officially the pantomime villain here in SASSYville), in whatever guise it decides to appear to you in – fear, resistance, lack of self-belief – will shout really loudly and try to drown out your real SASSY insight, so to make sure you're tapping into the real deal, take a step back from decision making and connect.

Go to the beach – the beach is the place I go to really connect. My heart feels soothed and at ease listening to the crashing waves and feeling the sea-salt air on my face and knotting my hair. I do really think I was a mermaid in a previous life, as well as Cleopatra too, obv. Wherever you need to be to connect and feel wrapped in love stuff, be there.

Listen to music – Now, in order to hear your intuition, you do really need to be still and meditative, but to make the initial connection, I really recommend listening to music. I am, and will be forever, in intoxicating love stuff with the *Eat, Pray, Love* soundtrack – I haven't felt this way since the *Moulin Rouge* soundtrack – I've lost whole hours in daydreams about how much pasta I could eat while surrendering to *la dolce arte di non fare nulla* – Italian-o style, listening to this album. It transports me to my happy place and when I'm in my happy place, I'm in a much better space to make decisions using my gorgeous all-knowing intuition.

Write – I know I'm a writer-girl and it's what I do, but sometimes I forget to use my skill for its magickal purpose, which is to clear out the head junk. I am a stationery queen and love nothing more than to fill up a pretty journal with wordage. I read Julia Cameron's *The Artist's Way* book a few years back and she encourages you to keep morning pages – 3 A4 pages, handwritten, each morning – it doesn't matter what it's about, you can repeat the same word over and over again, but the trick is, not to stop and pause. Just write. One endless stream of consciousness spilling out onto the page.

I've been doing it ever since, not every morning, although, I notice on the mornings that I don't, I'll be walking around with a fug of not-knowing above me, it will be like a *Glee* mash-up in my head, except with songs I don't like, and being performed by a really bad cast. But when I do it, it works, because as you open up to letting the words flow, you let go of all the insecurities, the fears, the worry and concerns to makes a nice big chunk of space for clarity and clear thinking. Writing – Feng Shui for the mind.

Get out of your way – my head seriously thought it was the big boss dude in the relationship it had with my heart. No matter how much work I did on myself, my head would put up the most almighty fight, it was like a freakin' warrior Princess, stepping in the way of any possible decision with armour, barriers and really negg-o 'what if's'. However, luckily for me, I am a super-hero-girl with powers o' SASSY, and I know that when I listen, and then go ahead and act on the heart-centred stuff, well… that's when the REALLY good stuff happens. All I have to do is just allow and trust. Now, I'm not saying I'm perfect, far, far from it – allowing and trusting does NOT come easy to me, but it is possible to banish the fug with these killer superhero tools – clear, heart-centred thinking and trust, and declare: *'if it's to be, it's up to me.'*

Regular connection can simply start by declaring to the universe/goddess/god/divine/spiritual homeboy-girl, and most importantly, yourself that you're ready to do this thing called spirituality, the more often you show up ready and willing and receptive to your intuition, the stronger your foundation for SASSY-ness will become. I mentioned it earlier, and I really do love ANY excuse to buy stationery, but a really helpful tool is to start a journal, writing down your gut feelings and what actions you did or didn't take. After a while, you'll notice a pattern of what happens when you do or don't listen to your gut.

Play your cards right

Apart from the Buddha belly rubbing, deep breathing and journal writing, another way that I connect with my intuition is to use the High Priestess card from my tarot deck. I am crazy-passionate about tarot reading, mainly because the more I learn; the less I realize I know. It's not all 'head scarf and hooped earring-wearing fortune telling at the fair', although I have been known to read for people in a headscarf – I do love a game of dress up – the tarot has never-ending depths and uses and they're a great tool for helping you understand yourself better too.

Depending on what deck you look at, the images may differ, but in most decks, The High Priestess holds scrolls of wisdom in her arms. She also has the moon crown on her head that indicates her willingness to illuminate what you otherwise might not see about a job possibility, an investment, love, career, family, etc. When you pull The High Priestess card she suggests that instead of making rash decisions, you need to take the time to listen to your inner voice. She wants you to gain knowledge before you act: instinctual knowledge, supernatural knowledge, secret knowledge, self-knowledge.

The High Priestess, however, goes beyond even that for those who seek more. Behind her throne is the curtain that leads to the deepest, most esoteric knowledge; the pomegranates that decorate it remind us of the Goddess Persephone, who was taken down into the land of the dead, ate its fruit and became the only goddess allowed to travel to and from that strange land. The High Priestess is our guide to all that is mysterious and mystical. She is my absolute go-to girl. I place symbolic reminders of her around my home, I have a card on my altar and have a picture of my favourite High Priestess card on my mobile phone, so that wherever I am, when I have a big question and I need to tap into my intuition to find the answer, I can use the High Priestess card as an insta-link to my place of absolute knowing.

Take some time every day, even if it's only for a few moments, to connect and listen to your intuition. Find a quiet spot where you won't be interrupted, close your eyes and relax your body. Take some deep breaths and relax your mind.

In this relaxed and quiet state, allow your intuition to come through. Give up one of your problems to your intuition and ask for help in finding an answer. You may immediately recognize your intuitive voice or you may not: everyone tunes into their inner self in a different way. You might experience strong feelings or you might not. You may have a flash of insight or your intuition may whisper sweet nothings into your ear. As I'm a Scorpio, a water sign, I always find my intuition is switched to loudspeaker when I'm in the bath, the shower, swimming, or by the sea. Try different places out for yourself and see what works for you. Be patient though, and keep practicing daily. Eventually, you'll be able to tap into your intuition, one of the most powerful SASSY super-hero-girl powers of them all, at any place and anytime. Wohhhoo.

Astro check yo'self

While some of our behaviours and beliefs are learned, or just stories we create about ourselves, other personality traits are part of our astro-girl make-up. Yep, how those twinkly stars in the night sky were aligned at the moment you were born can tell you a lot about who you are and why you do the things you do. I am obsess-o about all things astrology. I click on astrologyzone.com avidly on the 1st of each month, read Michele Knight's column each week and have Mystic Medusa delivered to my inbox each day, but the REAL juicy insight into who you really are can be discovered by having your natal chart read. You can do this online for free, you simply enter your date, place and time of birth, and it will give you an insta-print out of where the planets were, and which of the twelve houses they were in on your day of birth, but unless you know what all that actually means, (and having studied astrology for over three years I still struggle to even begin to understand it,) then I absolutely, positively recommend finding an astrologer who will do you an in-person reading. Your natal chart is like a blueprint for your life, it reveals and uncovers far more than just what your sun sign says about you and can help you to understand personality traits, why certain things have happened in your life and how you can use those traits and events to help you co-create your future o' awesomeness and attract people who are vibin' on the same SASSY frequency as you.

Good vibrations

Without getting too science-y, everything in the universe is made up of energy, and that energy vibrates at different speeds. Human-kind, us, vibrate at separate frequencies, and the thoughts we think, and the feelings we feel, determine the level at which we vibrate. For example if you've woken up in a grump, thinking 'today's going to be rubbish', you're going to be vibin' low, whereas if you've done a nice 20 minute meditation, sang at the top of your voice in the shower and smiled at your next door neighbour as you left the house, your vibin' will be sky high, which is super-cool, because our vibration goes out into the world, attracting energy that moves at a similar frequency. So when you're vibin' high, you'll attract high vibe-ers who continue to feed your high vibin' and you create nothing but goodness which others can't, and won't, fail to notice. If your vibin' is low, yep, you've guessed it, you attract the low vibe-ers and low vibin' situations, so that bad day of yours? It'll just keep getting worse. The good news is you can switch your vibin' to high at any moment by consciously choosing to focus your attention on the positive rather than the negative. To understand how powerful this is, take five minutes to describe something you love unreservedly, like a person, an experience or a movie. You'll feel noticeably lighter and more positive.

Keep raising your vibration by spending five minutes every day focusing on the good in your life. I write a gratitude list at the end of every day. Each night before I go to bed I have to think of at least three things that I'm grateful for. At first it felt quite hard, especially if I'd had a tough day at work, or an argument with a friend, but now I barely ever stop at three. Yep, sometimes you have to really search for the treasures in your day, but when you do, being thankful can sure make you feel lighter, and being lighter makes for much higher and happier vibin'.

When you wake, make the intention to notice more joy in the world, and watch how your day, and eventually, your life, is filled with it. When you take the time to look around and witness the beauty, kindness, wonder and laughter that surround us, what might have previously seemed ordinary and everyday becomes filled with the extraordinary. Sometimes I feel like my heart might burst when I see a sunrise on a cold winter morning, or watch the ebb and flow of the sea, or feel the kisses from my beau on my cheek as he leaves for work and I'm still under a nice warm duvet. If we bring this sense of delicious wonder to our lives, even for a few minutes a day, we begin to see just how blessed we are.

.... And breathe. Sigh.
Now, I thought meditating would be just like having a nap, and it is, but it's more like a 'working' nap. When I found this out, I avoided meditation for the longest time, mostly because it was hard. I couldn't stop the endless chatter, my mind would constantly wander to my to-do lists and I'd end up feeling more annoyed than when I started. For sure, the idea of meditating can be overwhelming, and, if you're anything like I was when I started, you might be a little afraid of what you might think and feel if you actually take the time to pay attention, but I promise, in that space between all the noise, there is all kinds of juicy, juicy goodness.

We often get so busy that the idea of taking time out to meditate just doesn't seem like an option. The thing is, meditation actually gives you *more* time, because it calms your mind, and a calm mind helps you to become much more focused. Meditation can also help you to transform your thoughts from negative to positive, from messy to peaceful, from unhappy to smiling-from-ear-to-ear happy. You've got to love that, right?

Don't feel like you've got to do it for hours, I can still only manage 20 minutes at a time, but the difference in my day because I've taken time to quieten my thoughts and breathe deeply is huge. Try it.

- Sit quietly with both feet on the ground and your back nice and straight.
- Start to breathe evenly and slowly in and out of your nose.
- Count 1-2-3 as you breathe into the belly, the ribs, and then the shoulders.
- Then 3-2-1 as you breathe out, from the belly, ribs, and then the shoulders.
- After repeating this for three or four minutes, your mind will feel more attuned to your intuitive nature. Listen to whatever thoughts pop up. If stressy thoughts of bills, or what you want for dinner come into your head, acknowledge them and simply let them go. I sometimes pop them into a pink bubble and send them off into the sky.

I'm not saying it's easy, because it's not. Meditation takes practice, but it's worth it. Gradually your distracting thoughts will subside, and you'll experience a sense of real inner peace and relaxation. When the incessant flow of your distracting thoughts is calmed through concentrating on your breathing, your mind becomes lucid and clear. Just by doing this simple breathing meditation for ten or fifteen minutes each day, you'll reduce stress and experience a calm, spacious feeling in the mind, difficult situations will become easier to deal with, you'll naturally feel warm towards other people, and relationships can improve too – hurrah!

The happy stuff

"I believe that the very purpose of our life is to seek happiness." -
The Dalai Lama

I don't often dig an orange ensemble, but I am a big fan of The Dalai Lama. The desire and search for happiness is one of the few things that we all have in common. No matter what race, religion, gender or political system you may find yourself splashing around in during your time on Earth, chances are you want to be as happy as you can, as often as you can, right?

Happiness has everything to do with the way you choose to think and feel about the circumstances that you might find yourself in, and very little to do with the *actual* situations themselves – so it's *your* responsibility to fill your life with as much happy stuff as possible!

My list of happy stuff is endless – spending time with the people I love, Paris, chocolate, kissing my beau, dancing, yoga, reading *Weetzie Bat* by Francesca Lia Block for the gazzilionth time, watching old technicolour movies, the rain, listening to Pink Martini's *Hey Eugene* album, getting snail mail and that's just for starters... I know this because they are all part of my happy-to-be-me box o' tricks that I pull out anytime real life gets a little bit too real-life-y and I need a shot o' insta-happiness.

I highly recommend making a list of your own that you pin to your cork board, or copy out into your diary or journal, so that when the bad mood blues comes to town, as they sometimes do, no matter how spiritual you are, you can send it packing by playing your favourite cheer up track, or taking a road trip to your favourite feel-good place.

What makes you happy?

....

....

....

Live in the present - easier said than done, but when you do, happiness is a near-on certainty. Why? Because when you wallow in past regrets/embarrassment/decisions that have been made, you'll just end up disappointed. The same goes for the person who worries about what *might* happen before it actually does – all this will give you is a messy, stressy head. Live in the now, it's not called the present for nothing y'know, it's a gift.

Do the things you enjoy doing – sounds simple, right? But so many of us deny ourselves the pleasures that fill us with happy stuff because we don't think we're worthy or deserving – stop that right now. For example, I get told all the time, 'Oh, if only I had the time, I'd write a book.' Now, not only is this incredibly patronising to writers like myself who really don't have a magickal set of extra hours in the world – despite what people might think – if you really want to write, you'll find the time. You want to write a book? Stop talking about how there's no time, and find time. Get up earlier, go to bed later, turn down a social engagement; just do it.

You are not responsible for making others happy, you are responsible for your own happiness - Sounds selfish I know, but you can't 'make' other people happy. Make yourself happy and the people around you will feed off the feel-good energy vibin'

23

that you exude as a result.

Travel as much as you can – travel rocks my world. I love to see new places, meet new people and experience new things, whether it's in the next county or across the other side of the world, broadening your horizons is a great way to step outside your comfy zone, realise there's more to life than the city you live in and flick your happy switch to the 'on' setting!

Of course, the knock-on effects of all of this are that everyone's happiness is affecting everyone else's happiness every day, all the time. So never forget, by actively seeking out your own happiness, you are actually increasing the happiness of everyone else on the whole planet – go you!

Is the grass always greener?

> *"The grass isn't greener on the other side, it's greener where you water it."*
> **Sharni – www.sharnanigans.com**

This simple phrase hit me hard.

When I split with an ex of eight years, I blamed him for absolutely everything. I blamed him for why I wasn't happy, why my life wasn't going the way it should and well... like I say, pretty much everything. Now, he was in no way blame-free in our split, not by any stretch of the imagination, but on my road-trip of self-discovery since, I have come to realise that only *I* can be responsible for *my* happiness.

Y'see, since I was a kid, I always thought that the grass was greener, I always thought everyone was having a better time than me, that they were thinner than me, earning more money than me, writing better books than me, having a better relationship than me, and that in comparison to 'them', well, my life was kinda sucky.

Which is why this life lesson really kicked my bee-hind. I really have found that the grass *isn't* greener on the other side; the grass is green and lush-like wherever I choose to put my love, focus and intent on a daily basis.

Here's how to cultivate your own patch o' lush, green loveliness...

No comparisons – don't compare your life to others. It's a game you'll never win. There will always be someone more rich, skinnier, better-looking than you, with a better car, more attractive partner and a bigger pile o' bricks – this does not, in any way, mean that you're not fabulous. Far from it. You don't know these people's stories, the only story you are author of is your own, so pick up your pen and start creating your life adventure on your terms, without the aid of comparisons.

Let go – Do you want love in your life? Don't let past bitterness and resentment from previous relationships or experiences stand in the way of you attracting someone new and fabulous into your world. Too many people hold onto the past with a super-tight grip, letting it effect potential future goodness. Have a letting go ceremony – I wrote a list of all the things that made me mad and sad about my past relationship, and burned it under a full moon. As the moon waned, so did my feelings of anger. By clearing out the icksville stuff, you're then able to clear some space for the good stuff to flow with ease.

Like attracts like – what you put out, you get back. You'll read that a million times throughout this book, it's the law of attraction, and most importantly, it works. To attract fabulous people into your world, BE fabulous. If you want to be loved, give love in huge, hefty amounts.

Cultivate – if life throws you a curveball, the easy option is to try and avoid it by running in the opposite direction, but do you know what? If you do, you'll always be running, as those curve-balls will continue to come 'atcha, it's how you deal with them that really matters. So your relationship is not totally rocking and ruling right now, that's not an excuse to go and get skirty-flirty elsewhere, no matter how carefree and fun that might seem. Instead, communicate with your partner, find out what's not working and find ways to help you both deal with, and feel better about the situ. Anything you put love and energy into, you'll love and respect a whole lot more.

Snap happy - When you're SASSY you can erase other people's yawnsville ideas of beauty and perfection and replace them with your own – I know, fabulous isn't it? Think of that nose-twitching witch, Samantha in the film *Bewitched*, except instead of changing things up with a twitch of your nose, you are capable of banishing negativity at the snap of a candy-pink, manicured finger. Who knew, huh?

This is how…

- Stand in front of a mirror with your eyes closed and think of a compliment that someone has paid you. Think about it in lots of detail, what did they actually say? How did it make you feel?
- When you feel all warm and fuzzy inside, open your eyes and check out your reflection in the mirror, love yourself up sweet thing!
- Now you're feeling all sparkly-gorgeous about yourself, snap your fingers. The finger snap action becomes an instant feel-good switch to your brain; so whenever you need a sprinkle of feel-fab glitter, just snap your fingers to activate your very own SASSY confident boost!

Goddess power

While I may not follow any one particular spiritu,
when I connect to source, I connect to the Goddess.

My spiritual homegirl.

The ancient divine feminine.

Embracing this awesome energy of lady-kind, is to accept all
that you are as a girl in the world. It's to live and love and laugh
and play. It's to celebrate and nurture your body, your beauty,
your creativity, your sensuality and sexuality. It's to care for
Mumma Earth, It's to follow your bliss, to have the courage of
Kali, defy the limitations set upon us by society like Freya. Being
with the goddess is to live a life of joy, beauty and freedom: of
compassion, nurture and acceptance: of honesty, integrity and
being true to all that you are. It's quite simply, owning and loving
your complete and total SASSY magnificence and stepping
through life to the untamed beat of your heart.

Because it's such a personal journey, you must find your own
way into the heart o' the Goddess and allow her to step into
yours, but to kick-start the goddess-girl love let me intro you to
my most favourite of all goddess-girls: Akhilandeshvari.

Akhilandaishvari: The never-not-broken goddess

I LOVE Akhilandaishvari.

When I first read about her in a feature written by Julie JC
Peters on Elephant Journal.com, I cried.

Don't get me wrong; Akhilanda is a total badass. For starters,
she rides a freakin' crocodile. She takes icky fear and borin'-
snorin' convention and gives them a one-finger salute. The thing
is, and this is the bit that made me make eye-water, she knows
that routines, no matter how comfy they can be, stop us from
growing. Akhilanda goes out of her way to remind lady-kind
that pain and risk are part of the breakthrough, and, that most
importantly, you do not have to be 'together', 'perfect' or truly
'sorted' to truly rock at this thing called life.

27

That g-friends, is true SASSY-ness, right there. Perfection? Nah. I'll take never-not-broken thanks. Think about it. Being never-not-broken is an endless opportunity to grow and start anew – how refreshing and totally liberating is that? Let me tell you more…

This goddess-girl from Hindu mythology, teaches us that, in *that* moment, you know the one I'm talking about when you feel lost, alone and in a Bridget Jones style heap on the floor wailing *'All By Myself'* at the top of your lungs, you are more powerful and full of awesome than you've EVER been.

'Ishvari' in Sanskrit means 'goddess' or *'female power'*, and the *'Akhilanda'* means essentially, 'never not broken'. In other words, The Always Broken Goddess. But we're not talking about the *'ohh, I'm so weak, poor me'* kinda broken.

Hell to the freakin' no.

It's the kind of broken that tears apart all the stuff that gets us stuck in a rut, a toxic groove, repeating bad habits and icky relationships.

Akhilanda gets her power from being broken: pulling herself apart and living in a state of flux, now that, seems like really freakin' scary stuff, doesn't it? But if you never become a fully sorted individual, and lets face it, I'm not sure any of us really ever do, or *should* for that matter, you'll never have limitations, and when there's no limitations? You have freedom. Sweet, sweet delicious freedom.

Any situation where our future, as we perceive it, is whipped out from under us – our heart is ripped to shreds by a failed relationship, a loved one dies, we lose our job, our money situ changes – is both daunting and terrifying in equal measures, because we all like the sensation of feeling comfy, of being in a routine, of thinking we know what's going to happen next – it's tried, it's tested, it's safe. So when that routine is thrown into turmoil, or we're forced to step out of our comfy space, we're left feeling… y'know, broken. The awesomeness of Akhilanda says, 'g-friend, when you're in this state o' flux, you've got a choice to make.' When you're on the floor, broken in little pieces, with no idea how you're ever going to pick yourself up again, you're in the absolute most delicious place of all, a place where you can start anew. YOU get to choose how you put yourself back together.

Y'see, life doesn't suddenly become really easy when you tap into your spirituality. Life will always throw you curveballs, but YOU are the mistress of your destiny. Don't let life happen to you, channel Akhilandeshvari and continually co-create awesome versions of yourself from the broken place of possibility.

Scary? Oh yes. Exciting? Abso-freakin'–lutely. In the words of Julie JC Peters *'in our brokenness, we are unlimited. And that means we are amazing.'* High fives to that!

Daring Dames

Like Akhilandeshvari, you've got the power to make your own Westwood heel-shaped footprints (or biker boots, or ballet pumps, or trainers – footwear is totally your call) but if you can find someone who's good at something, a role model, someone who kicks substantial ass in their chosen field, ordinary women doing extraordinary things, daring dames who aren't afraid to fly their flag o' SASS, then you can learn from them. I am obsessed with reading, and collecting, inspirational stories of women who are doing amazing things, they're a constant reminder that every day, someone, somewhere is overcoming adversity, is facing their fear, is taking a risk or is pushing themselves to become the very best version of themselves without compromise. My list o' Daring Dames is ridiculously long, and while I might not be able to get face time with Cleopatra, Joan of Arc or Boudicca, I am very lucky to have persuaded some of my very favourite 'living-right-now-and-doing-AMAZING-things' inspir-o-girls to share their own stories and insights about how to rock your SASSY, be authentic, speak your truth and become mistress of your destiny. They will inspire you, make you laugh, have you shouting *'hell-to-the-yeah, baby'* at the page. They are my gorgeous go-to-girls and I'm all kinds of happy to share them with you...

Daring Dame: Leonie Dawson

Leonie Dawson is beautiful, magickal and kick-ass. She is the epitome of a spiritual leader, she does her own thing, flies her freak flag and makes big money doing it – high fives and fist bumps to that, g-friend! She hosts creative e-courses, provides goddess guidance, creates amazing art – I have a piece in the Temple o' SASSY (my writer-girl room) painted just for li'l ol' me - and she writes an inspir-o blog that you should definitely subscribe to. She pours her heart into everything she does, she's real, she's honest and she's raw. Yep, I'm a fan-girl. And I will never tire telling you how much I dig her. Leonie makes me smile happy smiles right from deep down in my heart – come meet her.

You are an art-girl of awesomeness, yet you're so much more than that too, how would you define yourself in the world?

I'm totally a multi-faceted gemstone goddess. The moments I feel absoloodely at home on this earth are when I have paint on my fingers (and my skirt, and my chin...). When I'm in a sacred circle of women, handing a talking stick around, watching the moon rise over the horizon. When I'm making miracles happen and creating up a rainbow – whether it's doing an oracle reading or life coaching or creating art or a meditation CD or handwriting goddess guidebooks for my courses or blogging and sharing my soul stories. I feel like I have waves of coloured light coming off my hands whenever I do these things.

How and why do you follow quite so many paths o' creativity? Do they all fuel each other? Are some more important to you

than others?
Because they are all so ding dang glorious fun!

There isn't any that are more important than the other... it's all just one messy, glorious life of creativity and spirit. It's most important to me just to be happy, share my gifts and let the rainbows out however they want to appear.

You're a creative girl and a business woman - how do you do it? What gave you the chutzpah to leave your day job and make that happen?
A few years ago I got really sad that I couldn't do my creative & spiritual work full time... that I needed to have an office job to make do. And after I got sad, I got determined! Rar! I realised that I'd spent so much time building my creativity and spirituality muscles and hadn't developed at all my business muscles. I needed some business muscles in order to grow and support my big dream.

So that's what I did.

I read as many business blogs and books as I could. And I started applying them. And things started to really shift and work. I kept cutting back on my office job hours so I could keep growing my beautiful dream business.

And now?

Now it's my family's only job! My love and I are both stay at home parents to our daughter Ostara. We were both able to leave our office jobs and move across the country to a small town in tropical paradise here in Australia. I'm so so blessed and grateful that we get to live this magical little life of ours, but I know it wasn't an accident. It's one part inspiration, one part knowledge, and two parts work.

How do your own spiritual beliefs influence your work – do they inspire you to create in a certain way? Do they define the work that you do?

When I look at or read something I've created, I want to feel The Buzz. The Buzz that I'm looking at light, or spirit, or something beyond me. I want to feel inspired and uplifted and holy and like a goddess.

So that's how I create.

I don't create something so I can look at it and feel heart-broken or human. I create it so I can look at it and feel divine.

You're creatrix of the Goddess Circle too – can you tell us a little bit about that?
A few months after my daughter Ostara was born, I had a dream in the shallow hours of sleep between feedings. And in the dream, my guides told me to create an online sanctuary for creative, spirited women from all over the globe, and to give them everything I'd created, like my courses and workbooks and meditations and posters. They offered me this vision that the Goddess Circle would be giving everything I could to as many women as I could to help support them in their lives to feel like goddesses.

And it was kind of a nutty but gloriously wonderful idea. We moved across the countryside, and the week after we moved to Proserpine (the only town in the world named after the Goddess Persephone, coincidentally enough), the Goddess Circle was born.

And it's now this incredibly vibrant, sacred space filled with over 500 goddesses (at time of writing) from every continent in the world. Except South America. C'mon South American goddesses, we need you in there! We have Mongolia! We have Africa! We need you!

I get a real empowering lady-kind message from all your work, is this a deliberate sub-context that runs through your work?
I don't know if I have any deliberate sub-contexts in my work, more like faiths. I just know that joy is an option. That every

woman is a Goddess. That we can make our lives as beautiful and happy and glorious as we want them to be.

What do you love most about being a woman?
I love most that I get to be a Leonie, actually. I think we all get born to be ourselves. And I flipping love this turquoise adorned, mermaid-haired gigglesnorter that I get to be. That's my job in the world. To be the very best Leonie I can be.

Your bright and colourful work seems to be very representative of you, as I see you as a bright, sparkly, super-happy person, but I for one know how easy it is to wear a mask on the internet, Do ever have any self-doubt or issues that have got in the way of your flow? If so, how do you deal with this so you can do your gorgeous thing?
Sometimes I get cranky and jealous and obnoxious when I see someone else is doing something I want to do.

Then I remember that I'm here to do what I was born to do. It's not helpful for me to compare my soul to another's soul.

What does the term Goddess mean to you?
My patron is Goddess Leonie and my lesson this life is to listen for her wisdom and gifts. I feel like we are all modern day goddesses, just as important as the ancient goddesses. We all have our stories, our medicine, our wisdom, and our lessons.

What's your:
– truth?
Everything will be okay. It really, really will be. No matter what. You can sit deep in that faith.
– motto for life?
Joy is an option.
– secret to success?
Give it a go. Have faith. Try again.

– favourite go-to book?
Succulent Wild Woman by SARK.
– most treasured item?
The one I birthed. Ostara Faith Avalon glows like the most precious of stars.

You can find Leonie in these online locales:
www.GoddessGuidebook.com and in Goddess Circle at: **www.goddessguidebookcircle.com**

Moon power

In my home, there are two calendars on the kitchen wall, one for scribbling down what we're doing and when, and the other is a moon calendar. As girls in the world, we're ruled by the moon, it's the primary symbol for female energy, so it makes a whole lot of sense to chart its cycle, what with it taking about twenty-nine days to circle the Earth, the same amount of time as the average woman's menstrual cycle. Thing is, as members of this awesome tribe called lady-kind, we've forgotten the old ways. The wise women before us were in sync with the moon, their blood and hormonal cycle followed its ebb and flow; from new moon to full moon, estrogen increased leading to maxim-o fertility at full moon, when the moon is at her roundest and most abundant. From full moon to new moon, the waning half of the cycle, progesterone dominated.

Today, we're totally out of sync with its cycles, in fact we barely look up to know what phase the moon is in, let alone how our own bodies respond to it. You can find moon calendars online, I buy an Earth Pathways journal every year, which illustrates the cycles of the moon throughout the calendar year and what star sign they're in, these are all fabulous tools for getting to know yourself better, as they may give you clues as to why you're acting a certain way, or doing things the way you currently are. I started to chart my moods and realised that, like the wise women that have gone before, there was a correlation between my emotions, which are of course, water-related, and the cycle of the moon – we're connected, baby!

The moon cycles

- The Waxing Moon – when the moon is 'waxing' it's getting larger in the sky, moving from the New Moon towards the Full Moon. This is a great period of time to start new projects, meet new people, conceptualise ideas and attract new love. The period of the waxing moon lasts about 14 days.
- Full Moon – when the moon is full, she forms a perfect silvery sphere of gorgeousness in the sky. This is a time for 'getting it on'- you'll feel super-frisky, but just know, your fertility will be heightened too. Make like a boy scout and be prepared! The period of the Full Moon lasts from about 3 days before, to 3 days after, the actual full moon.
- Waning Moon – the waning moon is decreasing in size, moving from the Full Moon towards the New Moon. This is the perfect-o time to break bad habits or bad addictions, to end bad relationships. This is a time to really tap deep into your intuition.
- New Moon or Dark Moon – this is when the Moon is directly between the Earth and the Sun and therefore hidden. This is the a great time for planning new beginnings and new undertakings, while having a little 'cave time' to read, watch movies and pamper yourself.

Moon bath

I love to moon bathe. Right now where I live with the beau, we're on the top floor of a building that is south facing, so on the night of a full moon, if the sky is clear we throw open the windows as wide as they'll go and let the beautiful light of the moon goddess bathe us in our own boudoir. It's truly, truly a beautiful experience. If you're lucky enough to have a garden, lay down on a blanket, sit under her light and absorb her glamour. I have a necklace that I bought in Glastonbury, it's a black Obsidian stone wrapped in silver and I wear it as protection from negativity, to boost my powers o SASSY and because well, it's really rather pretty too. I charge it in the light of the full moon each moon cycle to give it an extra boost of gorgeous Moon Goddess power. Moon bathing is a beautiful act to do alone, and if you're brave enough and have a high enough fence, do it naked, it's the act of a true goddess and is the ancient way for lady-kind to recharge our SASSY powers.

Limit TV and computer time
To really recharge and connect, you need to disconnect from technology. Yep, you have to switch off the TV, step away from the computer and turn off Facebook. There. I've said it. If the thought of no techno-ness gives you palpitations, start by scheduling a day a week where you won't switch on your 'puter, TV or your mobile phone. Taking a day out from the incessant noise of adverts, news, messages to make you buy things and all things techno is a treat for your senses. We are literally bombarded with so many facts, figures, things to see, be, and buy, that actually, being able to think for ourselves and know who we are can be rather difficult. We can't re-invent the TV, but we can choose how much we let it influence our lives. If even the idea of a day away from your computer or social networking gives you the withdrawal shakes, at least make a pact with yourself to avoid it completely an hour before you go to bed. Try listening to relaxing music, sitting in the garden, read a good book, get craftin', write in your journal, meditate, dance – you decide!

My favourite way to spend a non-techno-day is to get me some nature time and fully experience the elements by going for a mindful walk. This involves being aware of each step your feet take on the earth, and also of your spine lengthening from the base to the crown. Imagine you are taking in breath from the ground, all the way up through your spine. There are few substitutes for a few hours walking in nature to help us reconnect with the earth. Choose a locale where you can fill your lungs with fresh air, such as ambling along a clifftop or through hills or mountains. You could also try a walk next to the water, whether it's a river, a lake or the sea, or you could get closer to the element of earth by walking among trees in your local park or woodland.

Wherever you decide to go, take a blanket so you can sit down, relax and enjoy your surroundings. Aim to find somewhere quiet and contemplative, then sit, close your eyes and meditate on the sounds you hear. Ahh... bliss.

Create insta-healing
I love Reiki, mostly because I can do it to myself. DIY spirituality rules. The word Reiki literally means 'universal life force energy' in Japanese and is used to release energy blocks, it's a truly beautiful healing treatment to give and receive. Guess what? While training to be a Reiki master will take a lot of years, you can activate your own healing super-hero-girl healing power o' SASSY right now, in your hands – ready?

1 Rub your palms together vigorously for a minute.
2 Hold your palms inches apart, as if you're holding a small ball. Is there a tingling or warmth coming from your hands? Now bounce your hands and feel the energy pulse as you move your hands in and out.
3 Hold your hands slightly further apart, as if you're holding a larger ball. Imagine in the middle of one palm is a circular area that can send healing energy. Rub this spot with the thumb of your other hand – you are opening up this area.
4 Repeat this process on the other hand.
5 If you want to send healing energy, you can hold your

hands over a part of your body, or a chakra, and visualise healing energy pouring in from the top of your head and streaming out through the healing spots on your hands.

Balance your imbalances

Your solar plexus chakra, found just above the navel, or in your upper belly, is home to your personal power – rarrr! – so if you're feeling a little out of sorts, that your energy is out of whack, or that you're not able to speak your truth, the ideal place to start looking for any imbalances is your solar plexus. A good healthy solar plexus will ensure that your confidence, self-worth and the ability to bounce back are good-to-go. However, if the chakra is weakened or becomes unbalanced, you experience physical symptoms, such as icky digestive problems, gallstones and indigestion. What happens spiritually is that you can fall into the victim role, unable to say 'no' or stand up for yourself.

Don't fret though, there are many ways to recharge your personal power so that you have the strength to crack your mistress o' destiny whip. Different things work for different people so make sure you try a few things until you know what works best for you. For many people, it's as simple as avoiding caffeine. Dehydration can also make your thinking confused and unclear. Whenever you're in doubt, take lots of deep breaths, open the windows wherever you are and get a good lungful of fresh air. Better yet, step outside and take five minutes to relax. Something as simple as fresh air can work wonders to help clear your head. As does writing down any negative or worrying thoughts that are bothering you. Seeing them down on paper can often make the difference between realising whether your fears are rational or not.

If fear is throwing your feel-good energy into a state of not-goodness, turn your 'fear' thoughts into positive statements of intent and say them out loud at least three times a day – use these to get you started:

"I am calm, confident and in control of my thoughts and feelings."
"I am safe and protected at all times."
"I am the power in my own life."
"I choose my own destiny."
I am good enough, exactly as I am."

Power Thoughts

If your mind is scattered and you can't find a confident voice within you, then you should definitely have a go at this power thought prompt. Sit or lie down and close your eyes. Place the palm of one hand on your forehead and the other on your solar plexus. Imagine your two hands linking your mind with your solar plexus, and just wait for any thoughts or feelings to come up. You may find some upset or issues slowly coming to light. If so, just mentally note them down, resolve to put your own needs first, and make yourself a priority, because you rock. Fact.

Enchanted space

I always thought that to meditate properly, I'd absolutely, positively need a meditation room. It would be white with flowy style curtains that blow in the warm morning wind. There would be a five-foot gold Buddha wrapped with a pink feather boa and there would be hundreds of tea light candles and twinkly music to create the most serene of spaces. This room is in a five-bedroom house in California, obv., it's a few minutes walk from the beach with a writing room that overlooks the sea and a hammock in the garden. Sadly, I don't live there... well, not yet anyway, but when you're SASSY it really doesn't matter where you live, it's *how* you live that counts. So open the door of where you're living right now, and fill it with magick and love-stuff. Here's how:

The hallway

This is a space for welcoming new opportunities. Place a cup of silver coins here to draw wealth into your home, and be sure to add a coin to it everyday. Stick a bay leaf to the inside of the letterbox to draw money through the door, and hang a wind chime over the entrance, its tinkle-y chimes will ring the changes of opportunities.

The bedroom

Invoke a li'l ohh la la passion in the bedroom by placing rose quartz crystals around the room, this is the room for romance, so make sure the first thing you wake up to is an image of beautiful heart-warming love stuff – I have the most beautiful piece called *At Last* by a super-talented artist called Yuri Leitch above my bed it's so deliciously sensual without being vom-inducing – and lighting yummy rose-scented candles.

The kitchen

This is where the nurturing and nourishing happens so the act of cooking itself already fills the kitchen with magick, but you can sprinkle even more by stirring your food in a clockwise direction to follow the path of the sun, empowering your food with lovely positive energy.

The bathroom

This is your room healing and relaxation. Whenever possible, bathe by candlelight, getting clean shouldn't be a chore, it should be an indulgent time-out from the routine of every day life. Use images of mermaids and sirens to bring in the healing, sensual spirit of the undines – the collective magickal name for the elemental water spirits.

The lounge

It's the party room, it's where the socializing takes place, so make this room inviting by burning oils that evoke comfort and famil-iarity such as frankincense, or sandalwood – mmm. If you've got people coming round, freely offering food is an ancient rite of hospitality so place a bowl of tasty treats on a coffee table for guest to nibble.

I think it's important to reiterate, that while I LOVE pretty things, I'm like a freakin' magpie to the pretty things, none of it actually matters. It's just stuff, even my pretty Vivienne Westwood heels that are so very, very pretty, they're just items I own. I'm SO much more than what I earn, or what I own and so are you. What *really* matters is the things we say, and the actions we take every day to fill our lives, and the lives of others, with as much magick, sunshine and most importantly, love-stuff as possible.

Make a SASSY playlist
The easiest and quickest way that I find to really connect and dance with my spirituality is to listen to music. It can lift your spirits, inspire you, infuse you with confidence, make you happy, and evoke emotions. I like to have a suitably SASSY playlist that will make me smile, dance, emote and feel ready for anything, now my favourite tunes change from week to week, but the tunes below are absolute fail-safe in evoking SASSY-ness:

I walk with the Goddess – Kellianna
Defying Gravity – from the musical *Wicked*
Girl Power – Shampoo
I hope you dance – Leanne Womack
Lovely Day – Bill Withers
Man in the mirror - Michael Jackson
Elephant Medley – Moulin Rouge sountrack
Walking on Sunshine – KC and the Sunshine Band
Like a rainbow – Rolling Stones
At your most beautiful – REM
Don't stop believin' – Journey
Waiting on the World to Change – John Mayer

's Greatest – R Kelly

'ling – Irene Cara

...nsuality – Bjork

Stand Up – Jessie J

What tunes would be on yours? Please share your playlists with everyone on the Sassyology facebook page – I always love an intro to other people's inspir-o tracks!

Daring Dame: Kelliana

Now this is one Daring Dame you will just fall in total heart-stuff with. Kellianna is a singer/songwriter who writes and performs the most magickal and beautiful mythology-inspired folk music and chants that sing to the goddess within us all. Her songs have seen me through many dark times and encouraged me to splash in my own gorgeous goddess-y goodness. Now, the first time I met this beautiful lady was when she made me breakfast at a B&B I was staying at in Glastonbury – one of the many, many reasons I love Glastonbury is that you never know when an international bestselling artist is going to serve you breakfast yums! She is a truly beautiful and inspiring goddess-girl and I do star-jumps of joy that she shares her talent with the world and I get to call her a friend!

Kellianna, when did you discover your musical talents, and how did you embrace them?

My first memories of music were of amazing female vocalists such as Judy Garland from *The Wizard of Oz*, Julie Andrews from the *Sound of Music*, and the Andrews Sisters with their phenomenal vocal harmonies. My mother is a music lover and introduced me early in life to a wide variety of music styles, from The Beatles to Bach. I remember when I was about 6 years old, we had this enormous stereo console with a turntable and I would spend hours putting on my mother's 45's and playing them over and over. I drove my parents crazy asking them to help me change the records, so they finally just showed me how to do it myself. I spent most of my youth listening to records and the radio and dreaming that I was Janice Joplin or Stevie Nicks, standing in front of my mirror singing my heart out. I started singing in the chorus in 3rd grade, and continued through my senior year of high school, where I was also involved with the theatre department and did several musical productions. The first band I sang in was when I was 12 years old, we were called *Medusa*, and no one was over the age of 14. We played rock n' roll covers, and were something of a local phenomenon.

I never stopped after that.

Twenty years ago, I dedicated my life to singing and for the last 8 years, I've been writing, recording and performing music inspired by ancient stories and sacred places. I always knew that singing was my greatest joy and never doubted that it could be my career. I always knew what I was capable of.

How would you describe your sound and performance style?
I would describe it as raw and real. A girl with a guitar, or drum, and a lot of passionate, powerful lyrics.

There's something very magickal about watching you work your charm on stage – can that 'confidence and charm' be taught or is that passion and fire intrinsically part of who you are as a woman?
I don't feel that confidence and charm can be taught, but it *can* be cultivated. The passion I feel for my music, and the passion I have for performing, are definitely a part of who I am. I think this passion helps define me within my genre. My fans appreciate the power of the music and the story, and I believe that my passion for telling the story in my way is part of what is making the music so successful. I made a conscious decision years ago to simply be myself when I perform. I want to be as approachable

and authentic as possible when I am on stage. I want to engage my audience and interact with them as part of the performance. I want the performance to feel as intimate as if we were sitting in my living room.

What do you love most about being a woman in the world?
I glory in being an independent woman. One who has made her own way in a niche that was just ripe for something powerful and new. I love the fact that I am my own boss and am able to make my own choices about my life and my career. I go where I want when I want. I work hard, and push hard, and then take a month or two off to rest, or to write. There is nothing more empowering to me than being able to call my own shots.

Who and what makes you happy, excites you, inspires you?
I live with my partner, Christopher Marano, and my Golden Retriever, Spike. We live a quiet life on a small mountain in northern Massachusetts. What makes me happy is to stay at home and enjoy the peace of the woods and the winds and the seasons. I live a very quiet life outside of my work. I'm a loner and a hermit who travels to make a living, so I am most happy at home, my place to rest and restore my energy.

What excites me is travel. I get home at the end of the year from touring and performing, take a couple of the winter months off, and then start craving another adventure. That's when I start booking my shows and travels for the New Year. It's exciting when music brings me to a place I've never been before. Lucky for me it happens all the time!

I think I'm inspired by nearly everything. People, nature, music, stories, love... life. Life inspires me. My own wonderful life, and the lives and stories of everyone I meet and have met. The stories of people struggling and overcoming and succeeding or failing. We all have them. Knowing people that have overcome their obstacles even when they seemed insurmountable helps me to push through the frustrating and difficult times in my life. It inspires me to try harder.

I'm inspired by the world around me. By the mountains, rivers and forests of my area, by the changing seasons and cycles of the year. The beauty of a sunny autumn day, the peace of a winter snow, the life of burgeoning spring and the joy of high summer. Each season holds so much power for me. I revel in the changes.

I'm inspired by my maternal grandmother, Delores, who left home in South Dakota at the age of 13 during the Great Depression, and moved to San Francisco. When she arrived on the West Coast she lied about her age and got a job driving a trolley car. She is one of the strongest, most inspiring woman I have ever known, and I am grateful every day of my life for her influence, wisdom and encouragement.

Can you tell me a li'l bit about your creative process?
My music is inspired mainly by mythology and magick. The stories of Gods and Goddesses from around the world. I draw from Celtic myth, Norse, Greek, and Arthurian mythologies. My obsession with mythology started young, at the age of 6 or 7, and was strengthened in grade school with a Greek Mythology class. When I reached high school and had a World Religions course, I realised that the stories that had fascinated me all of my life were born from the spiritual beliefs of ancient cultures all over the globe. My songs are often inspired by a piece of a myth. Many myths are very involved and complex, so I like to take a piece of the story, break it down, and tell the story through song using my personal interpretation. Other songs are inspired by the celebrations of the Celtic Wheel of the Year and by ancient sacred sites in Britain such as Stonehenge and Avebury, and in the United States, the Serpent Mound, and other Native American sites in the Ohio River Valley. Because of the amazing places and situations I find myself in, my music is heavily drawn from my

experiences.

I write very sporadically and intermittently. Often times I'll have a snippet of a song running through my head for months until I get it down on paper. Usually the lyric and the melody come all at once, and when I sit and write it down, I often find that I've created most or all of it subconsciously. I've written songs in a mere 5 minutes at times, others have taken nearly 3 years.

I do a lot of my writing while I am traveling, usually directly inspired by the sites and celebrations I'm experiencing. I write while gardening, washing dishes, driving, and daydreaming, but, I hate to admit, rarely do I sit and write unless I've been expressly commissioned to create a song or chant for a ritual, gathering, or special event.

What's a day in the life of Kellianna like?
Well, that is a question with two distinctly different answers. In my personal life, a normal day usually consists of sticking close to home and relaxing by watching DVDs or reading. I am a great lover of downtime, and have perfected the art of letting go of my demanding career for periods of time so that I can recharge my mind and body. I love to cook, and I love to make my space at home a comfortable, safe haven.

On a working day, I'm on the computer booking shows and travel arrangements for my tours, sending info and promo to the venues I'm performing at, and updating my performance schedule on my website and networking sites. I'll also ship out any CD orders I've received through my website. Then there is the nearly constant quest for new venues: festivals, conferences and gatherings. When I'm on tour, it's miles of driving from city to city, stopping at this shop for a concert, this town to teach a workshop, and arriving at a 4 or 7 day festival where I set up my camp and my vending tent for the duration to sell my CDs and merchandise. Normally at these festivals I'll do one or more performances and also teach a couple of workshops. The festivals are wonderful because now that I have been touring and playing these past 8 years, I've built a community of friends and musicians out there that I love to spend time with. These people are my tribe, and they make me feel at home wherever I go.

How does your spirituality impact on your creativity?
My success and international visibility occurred when I joined my spirituality and my music. I went from playing the same pubs and bars for fifteen years, to performing internationally in less than a year. For me there is no separation between spirituality and creativity. My music has become the vehicle for expressing my spiritual beliefs, and that is how I honour the old ways.

What has been your most magickal life moment?
The first time I had private access to Stonehenge with a group I was traveling with. We had gone to England to put a choir together to perform at the Goddess Conference in Glastonbury. We were in ceremony at Stonehenge, when we were sent off on our own for a silent meditation. I remember walking around those stones, my feet heavy as lead, so tired and so unsure about where my music was going. At the time I was in a band that was trying to write some songs and put a CD together, only nothing was getting done. I wanted out. I walked around Stonehenge asking the Goddess for guidance. What do I do now? Do I give up music and go cubicle? In that time of silent meditation I wrote the song Stonehenge, which was my call to the mother for her guidance. Two days later I was in Glastonbury at the Goddess Conference, witnessing all this amazing music dedicated to the Goddess, and I knew. I knew that was my future. It was all laid out before me. I went home and within 2 months I was in the studio recording my first CD, Lady Moon. I finished it before the new year, shipped a copy to the Goddess Conference, and was

wcase the very next summer. I feel that the one-
..onehenge, was the hour that changed my life. My
..e opened, and I saw a whole new world of creativity and
ρportunity. There was a brand new path, and I stepped out
upon it.

What's the best advice you've ever been given?

My grandmother gave me this advice: Do everything that you
want to in life. Don't be afraid to make your own way. Take
chances, learn lessons, and then take some more chances. Do
what makes you happy and be what makes you happy.

What's your advice for fellow members o' lady-kind?

Do what you love in life. We spend so much of our lives working
and making our way in today's world. If we have to work, it
might as well be doing something we love. If you've got a job, just
to have a job, but you have a dream of how you could make your
living, follow the dream. Make it happen for yourself. Do not be
afraid to step outside the box. With vision, persistence and lots of
practice honing your skills, everything is possible!

What's your life motto?

Dare to dream, and dream big...

See? Didn't I tell you? She makes my heart sigh the happiest of
sighs, so wise, so beautiful and so truly talented; I am blessed to
know her. To buy her beautiful music and find out more about
this lady of loveliness visit: **www.kellianna.com**

AUTHENTIC

"...And the day came when the risk to remain tight in a bud was more painful than the risk it took to blossom..."
Anais Nin

Know Thy Fabulosity

I am a huge slice o' awesome pie with a sizeable helping of amazing sauce on the side. There, I said it. And you should too, because blowing your own trumpet is COMPLETELY allowed. In fact, it's positively encouraged. Except you don't, do you?

Why?

Is it because you're worried about what other people might think of you? Maybe they'll think you're big headed or arrogant? Or worse still, maybe you don't actually believe that you're awesome in the first place? When you're SASSY, you don't play small; you dream big dreams and then you go right ahead and make them happen. Don't get it twisted, this isn't *The Secret*, you don't just 'think' good thoughts and expect the Universe to magically deliver all the things you've ever wished for. No, when you're SASSY, you bust some killer moves with the Universe. You see, the Universe really wants to do a cosmic two-step with you to make all your dreams come true, because it's rather good like that, but you have to make the first move. That's just how the Universe rolls.

Step into the spotlight

Start by shining a hot pink spotlight on your gorgeous self – scary huh? Unless you're super confident with extrovert Leo-like traits you'll hate the idea of being in the limelight, but I want you to think about the life you'd absolutely *love* to have. To really be able to awaken those dormant superpowers of SASSY, you need to know what you want. Not just that pair of ridiculously priced heels, although they can definitely go on the list, but what you *really* want. What does your heart desire? Be honest, be wild, be emotive, and most importantly, speak from the heart.

For the next hour at least, lose yourself in the endless possibilities. Don't read on and come back to this bit later. Do it now.

Write in your journal, draw it, create a dream board under the light of a full moon (this really works, I do it every full moon and fill it with intentions, quotes, pictures and words that I wish to manifest for the following moon cycle), record a song about it, blog about it, or if you're brave enough, make a video and post it on the sassyology facebook page. Whatever way you chose to record it, make sure you *do* record it, as this will be the map that will lead you to rediscovering the hidden treasures that lie within your heart and soul.

Take a deep breath, and envision your very own YOU-shaped land o' opportunities. What would it look like? Give yourself free rein to be as creative as possible with your desired life, and most importantly, don't let someone else's plans for you dominate, or get in the way of, your own bee-you-tiful vision. What do you see?

Is fam-time important? What about intimacy, amazing sex, heart cracked open honesty? Do you see your days filled with alone time, or shared activities with gal-pals, friends and children? Do you want to be paint-splashed, writing a best-selling novel or making big-ass money in a high-powered job? Do you see yourself in a cute cottage by the sea, or in a killer loft apartment in NY city? Do you see a life spent with one true love, or do you see yourself channeling your inner Parisian and entertaining a string of delicious-looking lovers?

How does that feel? To put your big dream life filled with all the people, places, feelings and thoughts out into the universe? Does it make you feel happy? Are you full of excitement or feeling a li'l scared and fretful? Record your feelings about the process too, this is a journey, and you'll want to be able to look back at them, in weeks, months and years to come.

Just so you know, your dreams aren't set in concrete; you can switch direction or change them up at anytime, simply have faith and trust that what's meant to happen, will. What's important is that right here, right now, you've given your big pumpin' heart o' love stuff a permission slip to dream, and this act alone will you get you an insta-audience with the Universe. When you record it, in whatever creative form you choose, you then show the Universe you mean business, which is really rather fabulous, because when our heart and the universe align, they do the cosmic two step, and we unlock the key to a SASSY superpower.

Atta girl.

What's stopping you?

So, come on, what's stopping you from making that big beautiful dream of yours a big beautiful reality? Is it a lack of money? Are you stuck in a job you don't like to pay the bills? Or are you just too tired and don't have enough energy to make the big dream stuff happen? What's your excuse?

Because that's all they are, excuses that stop you from being awesome. It hurts to hear that, doesn't it? But we seriously get in our own way when it comes to pursuing, and creating, awesomeness. We are our own worst enemies, yet instead of looking inwards and asking ourselves why we're being the evil Queen o' Life Sabotage, we blame external influences, because well, it's just easier, isn't it? That way we don't have to actually take responsibility for our actions and life can become something that just *happens* to us.

This is no way to live. I repeat: THIS IS NO WAY TO LIVE.

See? I even wrote it in capitals.

Look, I don't entirely blame you for wanting to stay in the cozy confines of excuse-making land, it's way safer than take-a-risk city that's for sure, but when you go to sleep at night, and you're filled with dread that tomorrow will be JUST LIKE

TODAY, I urge you to tap into that SASSY power of old, the fierceness of Boudicca and Joan o' Arc, and embrace your true fabulosity, because when you do, there is only one decision you'll ever make, it gives me goosebumps just thinking about it!

Through most of my twenties, I flirted between the two. Since my teens, I've had a connection to my SASSY super-hero-girl powers, except back then I didn't know what they were, I just knew that if I thought about something hard enough, like *'I want to work on Saturday morning TV'*, then did all the things needed to make it happen, like tell lots of people that's what I want to do, write to producers, ask people I know in the business for advice, that with a li'l bit of magickal chutzpah, they'd happen. In this particular case, my gorgeous friend Mark had a friend that worked as a TV exec, she agreed for me to do work experience on her show, I showed up, passionate and enthusiastic, and worked there for three years. Now, while I may have known about the whole 'thinking of stuff and making it happen', it's only been in the last few years that I've learned to harness the true power o' SASSY, to connect all five elements, tune into my Buddha belly sat nav and go forth with fabulosity. Before that, it was a little bit like that wizard dude, Harry Potter, having a super powerful wand and not really knowing what to do with it.

Y'see, I'd dream big dreams, then I'd sabotage them, because living in excuse-making land is safe and predictable, you know exactly what you're going to get, yet take-a-risk city is just so seductive, you can be whoever, and whatever, you want to be, but it's just so freakin' scary and fear-filled. In my early twenties, I was offered a presenter job on TV, and for a nano second I allowed myself to imagine how awesome that might be, so much so, I eagerly packed my bags for take-a-risk city, shouting *'look at me, I'm a risk-taking Rita!'* I told my family and one uncle laughed and said that they'd have to issue everyone with bigger TV screens if they were going to watch me, how else would I fit on the screen? Now, that one comment caused me to unpack my bag, decline the job offer and move straight back to excuse-making land. For years I blamed my uncle for missing out on that job opportunity. I even blamed other family members for not saying something to him, but actually, it was me who let someone else decide MY destiny. *I* made the decision to turn the job down based on someone else's opinion of me, but deep down, it wasn't anything that I wasn't thinking myself, he just confirmed what I thought everyone else would be thinking, so I used him as my get-out-of-TV card. His comment was the perfect excuse. That way, I didn't have to deal with how much I was actually hating on myself.

So, before you can move forward and start on the really, really good stuff, like unleashing your SASSY-tude, dreaming big dreams, making them happen and basically becoming the frosting on your yummy cupcake o' life, you need to know *who* you are.

What's *your* story, sweet thing? Check yourself for any icksville and un-lovely stuff, like fear and judgements that may currently be stopping you from moving forward. I know I know, I'm guessing your brain is making siren-like noises right now, that'll be because as humans, we're programmed to run like the wind when it comes to changing up our lives, which will explain why we often end up repeating the same negative patterns again and again and again. The thing is, if you always do what you've always done, you'll always get what you've always got, is that what you want? Do you want be an inhabitant of excuse-making land forever? You've got SO much freakin' potential, goddess girl, it's simply obscene that you're not rocking your most fabulous life. Now, in all my years as a coach, I've not met a single person who actually wants to 'do the work.' They'd prefer for us to hook up, TELL me what the problem is, pay me some money, and then expect me to provide the answers. That, however, is not how I roll.

This is how *I* kick it.

I am your gal-pal on your road-trip to awesomeness. I can provide the compass, point out some hot spots to possibly avoid, and turn the map the right way round, and I'll definitely wear a pretty ensemble and a head scarf, but it's up to YOU to drive the car boldly and confidently in the direction of your dreams and you can't do that if you haven't DONE THE WORK. You need to know what you're working with, and where you're starting from, in order to make any kind of progress with unleashing your SASSY super-powers.

FYI: I've read a LOT of self-help books, and the only ones that have *actually* worked are the ones where I've shown up and done the work.
Just sayin'.

Do the work
This is the deal.

Every single little thing you do is either taking you towards Destination Awesome, your life purpose, or away from it. It's as simple as that. Reading this book is taking a step towards it. If you put the book down and eat a family-sized bar o' chocolate, it's taking you away from it. Every decision you make, every person you choose to spend hang-time with, is either taking you towards awesomeness, or away from it.

So this is how I see it.

If you Do The Work, you're not just taking a step, you're running a freakin' marathon. You're making a huge-ass commitment to really get to know yourself, and when you know yourself, at a really deep level, you get all kinds of clarity, insight, direction, and confidence to REALLY take the reigns and become ̣ destiny! The thought of you rockin' a Boudicca-̣akes me beyond happy, just so you know.

Nitty Gritty Dirty Girl Time

Okay, let's do it, let's start by getting down and dirty.

What's the stuff that you'd just rather not talk about? The stuff that you want to brush under the carpet and pretend isn't happening? The stuff that brings you out in a nasty heat rash every time you think of it? What's holding you back? What's stopping you from dreaming those big dreams?

Take a deep breath and *really* think about it.

Is it fear? Do you think you don't deserve good things to happen to you? Do you see yourself as an unlucky person? Do you blame circumstances, like your upbringing, for you not being successful? Would your life be better if you were prettier, slimmer, had more money, lived in a bigger and better house? Whatever the reason, the most important thing right now is to be honest with yourself.

Make a cup o' green tea, set-aside half-hour alone time, light a white candle, and tap up the squirmy stuff.

Dare you.

What are some of the key words that come up for you? Does thinking about money make you want to put your fingers in your ears and go 'la la la' really loudly? Do you avoid opening your bank statements? Why? Every time you come up with an answer, ask yourself 'why?' Try not to think too hard, and just write down the first thing that comes into your head. If it helps, ask yourself what do these things look like? Do they feel like big dark overpowering monsters? What colours are they? If they were a character in a movie, who would they be? Really get to know these feelings and the situations and memories that you've attached them to in your past.

This is a tough exercise, which is why I suggest you only do it for half an hour to start with, that way you don't get too long to dwell in Debbie Downer land. The trick is, to identify the memories, thoughts, feelings and emotions that are holding you in that space, to recognise what they represent, and then summon up the chutzpah to either own them or realise they're no longer serving you and let them go.

But, hey, one thing at a time, right?

Life isn't meant to be hard. Honest.

When we arrive in the world, we are filled with nothing but the love stuff. We've got nowhere to go, no worries, no concerns, except one day, that person who's been looking after us doesn't come running straight away, they might have had to answer the phone or deal with a sibling, but to a child this is a BIG deal and we start to think we're on our own. We think that this being cute lark just isn't going to cut it anymore and that maybe life isn't so easy after all. A little bit o' doubt creeps into our mind and for the first time we experience fear. Grr.

Now, cast your mind back to when you were a child, and you wanted to be a nurse, or a ballerina or a vet or an astronaut. I'm sure you remember the response you got, right? I definitely remember those reactions. There was the art teacher who told me I really shouldn't bother picking up a paintbrush, so guess what? I didn't. The family member who said I was too fat to ever be on TV and oh, there was a friend who laughed at me for reading books who I totally ignored, because well, reading may be geeky, but it's my most favourite thing to do. Ever. The best one came when I said I was going to be a journalist. My school careers advisor said, *'Lisa, you've got to be more realistic. Those kinds of jobs aren't for the likes of you. You should stop daydreaming and start thinking about a real career.'* Negative comments and actions can knock your confidence faster than a ten-pin bowler, and you think this is how life is going to be, but living your life according to what other people think of you, is a serious waste of your time and energy and will hold you back from doing all the amazingly fantastic things you're destined to do. Yep, I was from a single parent family, and yep, I lived on a council estate, but that didn't mean I had to limit my dreams just because of my surroundings.

No way.

It may not feel like it, but YOU get to dictate how you roll in this lifetime. No really, you do. Yep, your life experiences might not always be sparkly and fun-filled, you may have experienced allsorts of not-nice things – loss, hurt, abandonment, rejection, heartbreak – and you may save them up and use them as ammunition to keep people at arms length, but you do know that doing this will keep fun, adventure and excitement to an absolute minimum, right? Your life will become very limited and incredibly boring-snoring. I know this because I've done it. Yep, this is where Li'l Miss SASS has to 'fess up. For a huge chunk of my life I had a very annoying voice in my head that I let tell me, on a near daily basis, that I simply wasn't worthy. Each day I'd wake up and my inner dialogue would go something like this:

I'm not worthy of a super-full bank account.
I'm not worthy of a hot beau who loves and adores me.
I'm not worthy of a healthy and fit body.
I'm not worthy of success.
I'm not worthy of friends who would do absolutely anything for me.
I'm not worthy of owning nice things.

Now, when you let it, negative chat like that can really ruin a girl's day. It's like a pesky downpour on a just-straightened hair-do. I'm really aware that the 'I'm not worthy' label was actually just a story I'd decided to believe about myself, and really, I was the only person who could change that story, but changing up our story is not easy. If it was, I'd have flicked the switch from 'I'm not worthy' to 'I'm freakin' fabulous and worthy of absolutely EVERYTHING I desire' in nano seconds.

It's just not that simple. Well, it is now, but it wasn't then.

You see, there's this pesky li'l trickster that I call the Funkatron. It's also known as your ego, the voice inside your head or other such titles that really don't matter, what really matters is that it has super senses that help it to know exactly when you're attempting to change things up a little bit. The Funkatron does NOT like change, and will instantly try to lure you in another direction, a direction that it thinks is much more comfy and safe for you, and jeez, do we love what feels comfy and safe. Y'see, our fall-back, manual settings are learned patterns of behaviour and no matter how they've served us, they're tried and tested, which ultimately makes them really comfy and safe.

I wanted to become a salsa dancer. Well, why not? It looked like a rather sexy and fun thing to do, and I wanted a li'l bit more fun and sexiness in my world so, I made the call to find out about classes in my area, which, at the time was a really big deal because I was overweight, I did zilcho exercise and didn't particularly like the reflection I saw in the mirror, yet, I was so determined to change things up in the life o' Lisa, that I even paid for my first lesson upfront. I was so proud of myself; I had taken the first step towards becoming a Super Salsa Sensation, now all that was left to do was meet a dreamy hunk o' Latino lovin', look hot in a red frilly dress and basically ooze sexy love stuff - my life was obviously about to change in allsorts of rather fabulous ways, right?

Wrong.

At the time, I let my life experiences continue to shape me, and when you do that? Well, that's when the Funkatron strikes. Hard. Its annoying Funkatronic voice in my head said: *'dancing? You? That's hilarious. You've never danced a step in your life. You do realise that you'll make a complete fool of yourself and people will laugh. And probably point a bit too. Don't go. Stay on the sofa, eat chocolate and watch the TV instead. Now that's something you're really good at that.'* My old patterns of comfort were about to be disrupted, just like yours absolutely, positively will be while you read this book, and my default setting took me straight back to the negative thinking and self-loathing. They were nice and safe, I let the Funkatron rule and as you've probably guessed, I didn't go. My dream of becoming a Super Salsa Sensation remained just that, a dream.

Would that happen now? Not a freakin' chance.

In fact, since becoming a girl o' SASSY, I've been to many a dance lesson, including Salsa. No Latin' lover, but I can totally ooze love stuff in a red frilly dress. So, what's changed? Well, I'm not going to say I don't still have a wobble, because while I may be a girl o' SASSY, I'm still only human, but if I find myself pinning the 'I'm not worthy' label to my chest, or letting the pesky Funkatron and its words of negativity win out, I now take a moment, and ask myself why. Not right away, because… well, I like a wallow as much as the next girl, but if a bar of chocolate and an hour-long 'poor me' convo with my gal-pal doesn't cut it, I go deeper. I ask myself, *what's with that? What's the connection? Was it something that was said to me as a kid?* A flippant comment from a teacher, a boy in my class or a family member, can take me right back to being eight again. Or maybe it was a story that I'd created based on an icky experience? Whatever the reason, instead of letting that comment or story continue to have power and shape my destiny, I now think of my negative thoughts and stories as a really crappy playlist that an ex-boyfriend might have made for me. Instead of continuing to play it and being reminded of how crappy aforementioned crappy boyfriend was, I now delete the tracks I don't like and download a new SASS-filled track in its place. For example, if your track goes a little something like this; *I'm never going to have money in my bank account because I'm from a council estate and my family has never had money*, it's time to switch it up. Start by acknowledging this particular story, because that's what it is, a story, and the best thing about your particular story? YOU get to write it. YOU are the author-girl of your own epic novel, the future is completely unwritten. Now, see, feel, think and realise how out-dated this particular story is. You're a girl o' SASS, anything is possible, so this is a no-longer-needed belief. Delete it and release it.

... And release

A good way to help make this process more powerful and juju-filled is to write the negative belief down on paper, then under the light of a magickal full moon, burn it to release it. As you watch it burn into the ether, chant a brand-spanking new belief like, *'I rock and I absolutely deserve, and I'm open to, prosperity and abundance'* and repeat to yourself as the old belief turns to ash. Let it blow away on the wind, check the direction of the wind first though, you don't want it blowing back towards you! If in doubt, flush it down the toilet to make sure it's gone for good. Now keep re-playing the new belief over and over on repeat as if it's your most favourite tune ever. In fact, whisper it to yourself before you sleep, put a tune to it and sing it at the top of your voice, actually record it onto your mp3 player so you can listen to it whenever you want, write it in lipstick on the bathroom mirror, keep playing it and saying it 'til you actually start to believe it, and you will.

The next time the same issue comes up, because sometimes it does, dig around and find another comment that someone has made, or a story that you have told yourself, and deal with it in exactly the same way. It may take a while, I'm still doing it, sometimes it feels we've invested too much time and effort with them to let go, but just keep deleting and creating a brand new, kick-ass playlist that YOU are in control of. If there's a track that doesn't make you want to dance or sing out loud, delete it and download one that does.

Digging into your past isn't always a pretty task, but in order for you to move forward and be a super-hero-girl o' SASSY you need to know why you do the things you do, so that you can either own them or release them. This is no easy task, and while this book is more than fabulous, I'd absolutely recommend working 1-to-1 with me, or any life coach, because when you deal with doubt, fear, judgement and disapproval you can really start to heal, and from a place of healing, ohmystars, you can do

freakin' ANYTHING, sweet thing!
Wohhooo!

Face your fears

*"...You gain strength, courage and confidence by every experience
in which you really stop to look fear in the face..."*
Eleanor Roosevelt

Fear is like the really obnoxious older brother of the funkatron.
It's sucky and not nice, but the most important thing to understand about that pesky thing called fear is that you *always* have a
choice about how to respond to, and deal with it. You can cave
in, struggle with it, accept it, or work around it. You always,
always have a choice.

Except, it's hard isn't it? Especially when they can seem so real
and scary, but when you know you've always got a choice about
how to deal with your fears, consider this. Think of fear as an
acronym for **F**alse **E**xperiences **A**ppearing **R**eal. Basically, FEAR
takes totally unproven stories about 'impending doom',
amplifies them, and presents the 'so-called' results as inevitable
failure.

Not cool.

Fear can seriously stop us from living our most amazing life.
The good news for you is that, as you collect and gather your
super-hero-girl SASSY powers there will literally be NO space in
your SASS-filled head for that critical voice that says: *'You'll
never succeed, so why try?'* Which is really good news, because if
we let it, fear could make us listen to those voices, and give up
before we've even started.

When you let fear rule your life, you can miss out on opportunities and dismiss people and situations that can help you live
a totally juicy delicious life of loveliness. Fear comes in different
guises and different forms – in the past, my fears have

manifested themselves most as procrastination. For example, when I was writing my teen book series, the first book in the series took a whole six months longer than I'd originally planned because I kept putting off the editing process. Y'see, editing meant finishing, and finishing meant putting my work out in the world to be judged. I'd make time in my diary to do it, then I'd decide to do the housework instead, and FYI: I do NOT love housework. I was letting my fears of being judged stop me from completing the one thing I'd dreamed about, becoming an author-girl. It's crazy, isn't it? I walked on actual fire to overcome my fears, it might seem a little extreme, but when you walk on fire, you find yourself asking, *'well if I can walk barefoot on burning hot coals, what ELSE can I do?'* it was an incredibly powerful experience and while I didn't know it at the time, it changed my life in a gazillion different ways. As I walked across the coals I let go of old hurt, old beliefs that no longer served me and cleared space for new and exciting things to come rolling in, and they have, and continue to, because that's what happens when you open your heart to possibility and face your fears head on. Now, I'm not saying you have to walk on hot coals, but if you're drawn to it though, you really should, it's one of the most amazing things I've ever done, it'll help you to put ANY fear into perspective.

I know how easy it is to want to stay under the duvet and avoid things that make us fearful, but just think of all the wonderful moments you would miss out on if you did, like, kissing in the rain – sigh, a beautiful sunset, a conversation that warms your heart, a smile from a stranger, a trip to a far-off continent.

A SASSY super-hero-girl, that's you, remember? Breaks through fear by doing the following: (hot coal walking is of course optional!)

Write down your fears – start by writing down the things that you're fearful of and how they affect your life. Write as fast as you can to block the Funkatron, your inner critic. Include EVERY fear, however small or irrational. Then read them aloud, suspending judgment.

Questioning your self-talk – Many of us don't so much talk to ourselves as make *actual* statements, like: *'I'll never be able to get that job'*. This stops your brain in its tracks and gives it nothing to work with.

Asking yourself questions – If you've got to stand in front of your colleagues and give a presentation, instead of instantly saying 'I can't do this,' ask yourself; *'how can I make giving this speech an enjoyable experience?'* That's better; now your brain has something to work with, see? Don't expect the answer straight away (but be aware of opportunities and situations that provide clues) Get into the habit of asking yourself questions rather than going straight for the negg-o statements.

There are NO mistakes – seriously, stop being hard on yourself, sweet thing. So, your last relationship didn't work out? That is definitely not a reason for you not to try again with someone who deserves your awesomeness. See your so-called mistakes as an opportunity to learn, and g-friend, you need to seek the learning in everything.

Recognise awesomeness – Know that whatever quality you like or admire in someone is lying dormant in you, just waiting to be discovered, developed and flaunted. How else would you recognise it? Make a list of the qualities you most admire in the people you dig, and ask yourself how you can tap into, and develop it in you.

Fears? Pah. There will always be moments, events and situations that make us feel the fear. The trick is to feel it and know that whatever it is, whether it's writing a book, speaking in front of a hundred people, or asking a hotster you've been crushing on out on a date, your fretful scared feelings are just a False Experience Appearing Real, so instead of thinking negg-o thoughts about what *might* happen, think about how AMAZING it could be – go on, I dare you! It's what a SASSY super-hero-girl with powers o' SASSY would do.

Just sayin'.

Go with the flow

To make sure you really address all those pesky negg-o core beliefs, dig a bit deeper. Y'see, they're ever-so sneaky and do all they can not to be found out. In fact, their very existence depends on your ignorance of them. If we just let them run, they rule our world.

To deal with my own negg-o thoughts and beliefs as they arise, I regularly practice automatic writing. Automatic writing is a form of divination in which messages seem to come out of nowhere through your hand and onto paper. I'm sure there's lots more important stuff I should tell you about what it is and how it works, but all you really need to know is that it's an amazing technique to get real insight as to what going on inside your head and heart. I do this every morning as soon as I wake. Take a pen and paper and set aside between 15 to 20 minutes.

- Find a quiet spot without distractions and sit at a table or desk where you'll be comfy, with paper and pen (or pencil).
- Take a few moments to take a few deep breaths and clear your mind.
- Touch the pen or pencil to the paper and try not to consciously write anything. While keeping your mind as clear as possible, let your hand write whatever comes across.

- Avoid looking at the paper; you might even keep your eyes closed. Give it time to happen (nothing might happen for quite a while).
- When it seems to be done, if and when automatic writing does occur, look over what your hand has produced carefully. The writing may appear to be nonsense or just scribbling, but try to decipher it as best as possible. As well as letters and numbers, look for pictures or symbols in the writing too.
- There's no guarantee that automatic writing will work for you, but don't give up if it doesn't work the first few times. Give it a chance. Let your mind unfurl, then take a look for repeating patterns. Over time you can identify icky not-nice beliefs and kick them to the kerb like the hairy, life-sabotaging monsters they are! You might also find clues for your dream-life too, the clues are there, they're in everything you do, you've just got to look for them!

Someone like you

When I was in my late teens I read a book called *To Be Someone* by Louise Voss. The contents of the book are kind of inconse-quential now, but I remember reading the title and thinking, Wow, I want to be someone. But what does that actually mean? Is it a list of achievements? Is it how much money you have in the bank? Or is that someone, simply me, stripped bare, listening to cheesy music, wearing outrageously pink tights with matching pink lipstick, and reading a chick lit openly on the tube without worrying that people are judging me? But, if that's the case, the stripped back version of me, couldn't actually be somebody, could they? That's just li'l ol' me without the Miss Perfect-o mask I've worn for a substantial amount of my grown-up girl life, and jeez, have I worn that mask well. I stayed in a relationship for far longer than I should have done because I didn't want to disrupt the so-called perfect-o life we'd created – nice pile of bricks, pretty garden, friends, jobs, blah, blah, blah – but I wasn't happy, he wasn't happy, yet we pretended to the world that we were. I kissed other boys, I'm not proud of that; he kissed other girls, yet we *still* stayed together. When we finally did split up, life was a big ball o' suck. I had books to write, books to promote, yet all I wanted to do was stay under my duvet and eat a family size pack of jaffa cakes. I still didn't tell anyone because I didn't want 'them', whoever 'they' were, to think I was a fraud. I wrote books about girl power and all things positive, yet inside, I felt completely the opposite.

I wore that mask right up until I met my beau, the man I'm going to marry, and he instantly saw right through it, he looked right past the mask, deep into my soul, saw that I wasn't perfect, in fact, I was far from it, I was at my heaviest and I wasn't dealing with any of the emotional 'crap' that was going on beneath the mask, yet he loved me anyway, and he continues to love me right up every single day, it's all kinds of beautiful. To be that loved and accepted motivated me to sort out the emo 'crap' and drop the mask.

Jeez Louise, it's so unbelievably liberating to not be Li'l Miss Perfect-o anymore. When you're just being yourself, no acting, no faking it, life is so much freakin' sweeter. For sure, it definitely leaves you vulnerable, because there's nowhere to hide. What people see, is the real, uncensored, unapologetic, not-perfect, but still-so-deliciously-gorgeous you. But it's super-powerful too. It's like flying a flag o' SASSY at full mast and declaring, '*I'm me, and I rock!* If *Dancing Queen* comes on in the post office while I'm queuing, I'm going to dance, that's just how it is now. I end every email, whether it's to my beau or my bank manager, with: '*love and cupcakes, Lisa x*' If I don't want to do something, I no longer try to think up an extravagant excuse, I simply say 'no'. I wear ridiculously over-the-top and brightly-coloured accessories. When I bring my SASSY-flag-flyin' self to the table, life is good.

To be 'someone' is to simply be me, beautiful, imperfect me.

What masks are you wearing? List all the masks you are currently wearing and what they represent to you...

....

....

....

What will happen if you drop them? Who is under those masks? What beautiful qualities will you unleash on the world?

....

....

....

Who am I?

Life is a whole lot easier when you know who you are. Now, I am big on making life easier wherever I can because struggle often involves sweat, and I do not like to sweat.

Do you know the real you? What does she look like? Do you take time to connect with her? How real do you think you are? Who do you let, if ever, see the real you?

Now we are all capable of flicking our 'make them like me' switch in social situations, because we want people to feel at ease with us, and we want to get on in life, make friends and build professional contacts. So it just seems like the right thing to do. At school, I used to often find myself agreeing with people, mainly because I didn't know what I really, truly felt, so it was easier to just smile and agree than to actually think for myself. When I realized that the 'smile and nod' behaviour was an insta-link to making them like me, I kept doing it, right through to early adulthood. If it's not broke, don't try and fix it, right?

Wrong.

While this was happening, the 'real' me was curled up in a little ball, somewhere deep down in the bottom of my belly. It made itself known though, every time I flicked my 'make them like me' switch, which in my early 20's was pretty much all the time, I'd get chronic tummy aches, I went to the doctors, but all he could suggest was a bottle o' Gaviscon. It wasn't until I started to wonder why life wasn't quite turning out how I'd imagined it, and asking myself why is that, exactly?' that I slowly began to realize I didn't know who I was. Until that point, I was a combination of friends and families thoughts, feelings and opinions and what I'd read in *Look-in* and *Just Seventeen* magazine. I felt like I was about to embark on some mammoth re-invention a la Madonna. I started asking myself who do I want to be? What do I dig about that person? And that was a fab place to begin, because being inspired by, and adopting the characteristics of people you admire to become who you want to be, and express who you are, is definitely a prerequisite to awesomeness, but true world-shaking, super-hero-girl, revolution-starting awesomeness can only occur if it's being done from a strong, solid core. Your very essence of being.

Have you ever heard someone say, 'this is my calling' when describing their dream job? Or 'my mission in life is to fulfil my purpose?' The feelings they're experiencing are coming from their core, their centre of being. It's like those sticks of candy rock that you can buy at the seaside, you know, the ones with their location running right through their middle? Well, we're exactly the same, crack us open and you'll reveal our inner core running right through the centre. One of my favourite poets, Rumi said: *'Everyone has been called for some particular work, and the desire for that work has been put in their heart.'*

I don't think he meant work in the 9-to-5 sense, I think he

meant in terms of life work - your passions, values, desires – the things we so often push aside to do what we think we 'should' do.

Your values represent that big, beautiful essence o' yours, so it's kinda important that you know what they are. Some you will recognize straight away, while others will only make themselves known in times of change, or circumstance. What must you absolutely, positively have in your life in order to feel full-to-the brim and satisfied? I don't mean the basic stuff like food, and a roof over your head, what are the things you absolutely must honour or else you'll feel incomplete?

Over the next couple of days and weeks, be open to what those values are. Ask the universe/divine/spiritual homeboy/girl for guidance, in fact, if you listen to your body, it's a beautiful compass for your core.

My belly is my core's GPS system, and when I'm off track and not being true to my core values, my tummy will always let me know.

Some possible values might be:
Integrity
Beauty
Honesty
Joy
Happiness
Excellence
Lust
Peace
Harmony
Truth
Love
Tradition
Independence

At my core, my values are simple:

- Spirituality.
- A need to be real, have 'real' experiences, share 'realness' and surround myself with people who are 'real'.
- To express love in all forms – to myself, through my work, to others, to the world, to the universe, infinite.
- To know, and own, my personal power and help others discover and own theirs, so they can go do awesome things in the world.

The clues to your destiny are all there for the taking, you just have to make like a detective girl, and look for the clues. You can wear a deerstalker if you like, but unless it comes in pink, I'll pass, ta very much. Sometimes the clues are right under your nose, or other times you may need to look to your past – what were you up to when you were younger? When life was a li'l more carefree and easy, what did you love doing? How did you express yourself? Or how would you have expressed yourself if you'd known how? After spending so long not being real, it makes so much sense that one of my core values is to actually be real, doesn't it? I wrote that list above, in my diary, the day before New Years Eve in Paris, which is also when I conceptualized SASSY, but back then it was just a word, one of my favourites, and a word often used to describe myself and my bestie, Miss Aimee, so I owned it, I bought a name necklace with it on, and wore it as my power word, and when I did, the magick happened. You know why? Soon after, I was scribbling the word SASSY and started writing a meaning for each of the letters, within minutes, SASSY stood for Spiritual, Authentic, Sensual & Sensational You, a combination of ALL my core values and a few months after that, it became the perfect way for me to help lady-kind discover their own SASSYness through coaching, magick and make-life-better-ness. When I made that realization of epic awesomeness, it was as if the sparkly Eiffel tower in my snow-globe heart was putting on a light show just for me, and anytime I ever see it now, in a picture, or real life, I imagine it as my core essence – a strong, beautiful solid structure that sparkles and shines and brings happiness to all those who are ever in its presence – voila, et moi!

So, who are you, sweet thing?
You are who you say you are and the good news? You get the final say. Of course you can play at it, try a few personas out for size or simply fake it 'til you make it, but how about instead of wasting time with all the bullshit, you crack open your beautiful essence and share who you really are, what you're really here for, with the world. Yep, this takes a whole lot o' chutzpah and go-for it girl juice, but the pay off?

Wowzers.

Let me tell you, the pay off will blow your freakin' mind.

First off, you will know who you are, what you stand for, and what you were born to do so deep down in your bones that you'll find yourself skipping down the street, whistling a song for no reason, and smiling your 'I've just had sex and it was ah-freakin'-mazing' smile. You'll have the most incredible knowing that all the wise women, the girls o' awesomeness, the goddesses o' deliciousness who have gone before, trod their own path and spoke their truth did not do so in vain – high fives to that. You won't need to go on a super-expensive, find-yourself retreat, unless you fancy it, obv., and most importantly, once you know yourself and your extreme fabulosity, you'll recognize yourself anywhere. It's the ultimate in personal power, you'll never feel inferior or not good enough ever again. When you make a decision, you just check that it's in alignment with your core values, and you're good to go. You won't ever feel like you don't belong and you can go anywhere without getting lost because your compass will always be set to your North star, your heart.

Fly your SASSY freak flag

"...I don't judge others. I say if you feel good with what you're doing, let your freak flag fly..."
Sarah Jessica Parker

Seriously, life becomes a beautiful shade o' sweetness when you fly your flag o' SASSY, love makes your heart thump ridiculously hard and you are surrounded by a gazillion cartoon hearts at all times, work and business thrive, you can tap into your creativity a whole lot easier and most importantly, you unlock another key to your SASSY super-hero-girl powers – ka-ching!

Much to my parental's disappointment; I've got beautiful tattoo ink splashed all over my body. In fact, if I weren't such a wuss, I'd be covered from head to toe in art. I love how I feel when I look in the mirror and see parts of my life, memories and experiences captured forever on different parts of my body. I know that not everyone digs the ink, but for me, it's a beautiful way to express who I am to the world.

Other less permanent ways to fly your flag o' SASSY include:

No comparisons – stop worrying about what other people 'might' think, don't ask yourself if so-and-so will like it, instead ask yourself, *'do I like it?'* You do? Awesome sauce. Now go right ahead and do it.

No holds barred – if, like me, you like to use slightly out-there vocab, do it. I wear a huge-assed pink flower in my hair and tell people it's an antennae for creative thoughts, clash colours in your wardrobe, wear a leopard-print slanket like a cloak o' power, answer the phone speaking nothing but French for a day, paint each toe-nail a different colour... the world is your clam. Or oyster. Whatever.

Tune into your magickal mojo – what do you want to do do you want to be? Tune into your magickal mojo, listen t heart really closely and follow it wherever it takes you...Maybe it wants to listen to live music, find a venue in your area that showcases new bands and go listen, you may meet new like minded people, you might be inspired to play tambourine, who knows? Fill up your magickal well with gorgeous goodness and see where it leads you!

Surround yourself with flag o' SASSY flyers – you can meet them through the SASSYology Facebook page, you can meet them in real life, they're the people who will be smiling from ear-to-ear and shining a light o' love and positivity from deep in their hearts. I'm lucky to have a lot of friends in Glastonbury, one of my most favourite place in the whole wide world, mainly because there are allsorts of flags flying there and they're all freakin' fabulous. Nowhere else in the world would I have walked up The Tor in a designer dress (Matthew Williamson, if you're interested) worn PJs down the high street, a leopard print witches hat and cloak to Challice Well Gardens and immersed naked in the White Springs – the gorgeous people o' Glasto actively encourage my flag flying, and I encourage yours, wave 'em, baby!

Stand up

> "...To acquire true self power you have to feel beneath no one, be immune to criticism and be fearless..."
> **Deepak Chopra**

High fives to that, Deepak, except what you forgot to stress was how challenging that can sometimes be. It takes real courage to live life truly out loud, fly your freak flag and to do what you were born to do, which is why so many people don't. Instead they get crazy-rage bitter and when they see people who are rocking out at their best life, they criticize and find all kinds of fault. The worst culprits? Other women.

This makes me want to beat a pillow hard and cry big, ugly tears, because I want so much for this not to be the case. Women play the comparison game with each other, which FYI, is the silliest game of them all because sadly, there's never a winner. There will ALWAYS, and I repeat, always, be someone who's taller/shorter/thinner/curvier/paid more/has a bigger house/newer car – delete as applicable – than you. It's fact. Yet every day, women all over the world are playing a game they cannot win and hating on themselves, and each other, because of it. Some girls express their frustration and anger by vocalizing it directly to the source, or bitching about it on a blog or a magazine column, which in a way, I admire because at least they're vocalizing it. The worst kind of criticism, and this makes me beyond sad, comes wrapped in ick-y sugary sweetness. The angrier these girls get at not measuring up to their friends/celebs/models best life, often the sweeter they act. I don't blame lady-kind for either response, as women we're simply not taught how to express our thoughts and feelings honestly, we're simply playing by a set of rules passed down through recent generations. When we're at our worst, many of us exclude other women so we can feel more important than them, back-stab our friends so others will see us in a better light and vie to be the special one, forgetting that we are special.

This behaviour is not serving the world, our relationships with fellow lady-kind, or ourselves. No one is to blame, but let's not make excuses either, we need to be the change we want to see in the world so I challenge you to be honest, rather than saying what you think others want to hear. I challenge you to not compare yourself with other women, but to notice the beauty in each other and compliment, and celebrate, that. I challenge you to ask for what you want, rather than using manipulation to get it. I challenge you to be yourself without stepping on fellow lady-kind in the process. I challenge you to join together to channel your SASSY-ness and wrap your arms around the world in one huge-ass, hug o' love.

For that to happen, we have to dare to step up and not only *know* ourselves, but to *be* ourselves too, because if we don't, we will continue to have to get our needs met through manipulation, mixed messages and deception and it will be lady-kind who continues to pay the price, simply because we're too scared to be authentic.

I am NOT cool with that.

Rock the chutzpah

"…To be nobody but yourself in a world which is doing it's best, night and day, to make you everybody else means to fight the hardest battles which any human being can fight; and never stop fighting…"
E. E. Cummings

Which is why, chutzpah, courage, go-for-it girl juice, whatever you choose to call it, is an absolute essential, must-have requirement in your vanity case o' SASSY-ness, and just so you know, you're going to need it in abundance.

That doesn't scare you does it? It shouldn't, what's more scary, is living the life of that well-behaved woman, the one who's sugar-y sweet on the outside, and a ball of rage, anger and resentment on the inside. As American historian, Laurel Thatcher Ulrich, so rightly pointed out, *'well-behaved women seldom make history'* and we, gorgeous lady o' SASSY-ness are writing our own legend, right here, right now, so that all members of lady-kind who we speak to, and connect with, cannot help but feel, and want to be a part of, the juicy deliciousness that is a revolution-starting woman living in her

r. Wait, you did know that you were starting a
dn't you?

...i the SASSY girls do, y'know.

It will mean though, that from time to time, you will have to deal with criticism. Hence the need for industrial strength chutzpah. Oh, and a helping hand from the gorgeous Goddess Leonie. I have not found a better way to deal with critics than this, which is why I shameless stole it for my vanity case o' SASSY, and because that gorgeous girl is SASSY-ness personified, she's more than happy for me to share the love stuff with you too – hurrah for Leonie!

How to Deal With Critics – Goddess Leonie style

"...Ignore anyone's advice/criticism/judgements unless they are genuinely happier than you.

I haven't been in a circumstance yet when someone criticising me is actually happier than me.

SO I WIN. YAY!

That's my two-second answer.

Want my forever-long story that has a bit of swearing in it?
I got judged and bullied when I was a kid. When I was 15, I got so fed up with being bullied for being me, I informed my parents that I was either going to send myself to boarding school or go and be an exchange student. I ended up choosing to go to a wonderful little country boarding school where I very happily spent the next two years swimming in quiet waters. Yay! No bullying!

But here's the thing I learned.

It's a very special motto:

FUKEM.

If you say it quickly enough, you'll hear my sacred saying.

The thing is...

I really bloody LOVE being Leonie. I make me happy. I like my quirks and my silliness and who I am. I dig that my brain doesn't work like many other peoples.

And I don't want to be like anyone else. Especially boring people who judge me.

I LOVE my little life.

And I have a blatant disregard for anyone who doesn't love me. I think "ummm... well aren't you a bit daft then! I'm awesome! Okay then! I'm off to keep dancing!"

If people don't get it, it's cool by me. Because what I am and what I do makes me totally happpppy.

So...

FUKEM.

And I get to hang out with people who DO get it and get me (nearly most of the time) and they are the kind of peeps I want to hang out with.

(Also, as an aside... you know what happens quite often when you think someone doesn't get it or doesn't love you? They often come to their senses much later. Like I've had a number of people I lost contact with who I thought just didn't adore me anymore... and they've found me later on and said "Leonie, I really need to tell you how much a blessing you were in my life... thank you for everything... even when I didn't get it...")

And I totally believe that all of life is like that. We all see each other's beauty eventually. *Just give it time. And in the meantime, carry on having a freaking amazing time being you..."*

I could not love this woman more. Love x 10000.

So, chutzpah, how do I get me some o' that?

Just a heads up, courage doesn't make you fearless, but it is the go-for-it girl juice you need to drink on a daily basis to give you the strength to be who, and what, you are - despite your fear. You ever hear the phrase 'feel the fear and do it anyway?' That's what courage is, knowing your fears, being aware of them, but going right ahead and starting that revolution anyway.

You can flex your chutzpah muscle by:

- Recognizing your fear. Don't make excuses and call it something else, because you can't overcome it, or move through it, if you don't recognise it. Fact.
- Let fear be your teacher. At the school o' SASSY Arts, fear is most definitely our biggest teacher. Ask yourself, what am I basing this fear on? We experience fear when we believe the lies that we tell ourselves. What do you believe to be true?
- Commit to Courage – life rewards action remember, you're not a well-behaved woman, you're a super-hero-girl with a vanity case o' SASSY super-powers, so you can take risks, in fact I positively insist that you do. The more risk your take the stronger your chutzpah becomes, it's how revolutions start. Just sayin'.
- Celebrate and honour your ever-growing supply o' chutzpah – every time you face a fear and take a risk, you must acknowledge, celebrate and honour it – light a candle, do a happy dance, take a picture to remember the day and put it in your journal with the heading *'I am awesome!'*
- Chutzpah is built one success at a time. You are successful every time you try – know it, own it.
- Trust your intuition/your compass/your spiritual homeboy/girl: check in. You know that guidance is available to you, because you've experienced it, right?

Take a life inventory

"...Happiness is when what you think, what you say, and what you do are in harmony..."
Mahatma Gandi

I know the idea of sitting down and talking a long hard look at your life may seem freakin' scary, and that's because, for the most part, it is. Looking at the things that are working and aren't working in your life, in a completely honest and frank way, *is* scary. It's also the most liberating experience you'll ever have and I absolutely, positively promise that after doing it, you'll be doing a trillion star-jumps of joy.

I know it'll be really tempting to skip this bit of the book, promise yourself you'll come to it later, or flick to the pages about sex and all things ohh-la-la, but if you're super serious about leading a SASSY life, reaching your most beautiful potential, dreaming big dreams and making them happen, how about you girl-up, and right here, right now, make the decision to get real. It's not about passing judgment on you, your life or the decisions you've made in it, nor is it about giving yourself a big stick to beat yourself with either. Being real with yourself is your opportunity to make the path to awesome a little less stressy and easy on the feet, because if like me, you're walking this path in killer heels, you're going to want that terrain to be as smooth as possible, right?

So basically, this is how it works.

Sometimes you have to go back to your past to create the future. Ever since I was 14, and I earned my first wage working in a local newsagent, my relationship with money was substantially sucky. I came from a family where we didn't have much, so to actually have access to my own money at the end of each week was the stuff of dreams. Except, I had no idea what to do with it. They don't teach you that stuff at school. No sooner had I been paid, I wanted 'stuff' to show for it. I bought magazines and sweets and surrounded myself with them until I got paid the week after and did exactly the same thing. It was as if I needed proof of my worth and the money itself wasn't enough, I wanted stuff, things to show for it. My bestie was completely the opposite, she too came from a family who struggled with money, but when she got paid, she saved. And then saved some more. It was as if she was too scared to spend it, just in case she never got any more, where as I on the other hand, needed material proof to show that I'd actually had it. This pattern continued until I took my own life inventory LAST YEAR. Yep, despite my love of all things self-help-y, reading book after book about improving my life, all of which were perfectly fabulous and full of delicious ways to make my life better, easier, more successful, nothing really shifted until I got real with myself. It wasn't until I took my own life inventory, inspired by a feature in a magazine, that I realized my relationship with money was affecting my relationship with... well, pretty much everything. Financially, I'd messed up big time, and if you've ever been in the position where you've had bills to pay but didn't have any idea how you were actually going to that, you'll know that it affects the way you go about living your life. That's if you actually open the bills and not hide them in books, hoping and praying they'll go away. Yep, that was me too. For sure, you can paint on a smile, and fool yourself that the bills don't actually exist if you don't open them and hide them in aforementioned book/drawer/hiding place o' choice instead. Yep, me again. But if you have done that, you'll also know that it's sucky. On an energy level, your vibration is low, and despite any sunny disposition you're able to muster, subconsciously, you're sending out 'I'm a bit rubbish' vibes, which means you attract similar people and situations into your world of low vibrational sucky-ness and that becomes your mirror, so when you do feel brave enough to take a look at yourself, you just don't love what's staring back at you. This can make you feel icky about yourself and that attract icky-ness in all its forms - bad food, bad people, bad relations, bad luck. My poor relationship with money had thrown my sense of worth in life completely out o' whack, and it had a direct impact on the food I put in my body, the relationships I found myself in, everything.

If I hadn't taken that life inventory, I'd still be operating from a place of un-SASSY and that would be, quite simply, the worst. I mean it, if there's only one exercise in this whole book that you do, make it this one. It could literally change your life. I know big sweeping statement, right? But seriously, in order to go where you want to go - the directions of your dreams: Awesomeville – you need to know where you're at right now.

To make this process as pleasurable as possible, and I am all about the pleasure, take yourself on a date. Dating myself is one of my favourite things to do – an art date, a pamper date, a nature date – any kind o' date that involves you spending time with the most important person in the world - that's you, by the way – is a date well spent. Fact. Load yourself up with pretty stationery, felt tip pens, buy a new journal for the occasion, and take yourself to your happy space, mine is The Art House, a gorgeous arty café in town, where they serve yummo food and have mis-matching furniture, if you're going out in nature, make sure you take provisions, if you're in a café, order your favourite beverage and yums and then take deep, deep breath.

You're doing this and I'm so freakin' proud o' you.

Now, I know a life inventory sounds all terribly big and grown-up, doesn't it? I tried to think of a million different names for it, but sometimes you've got to keep it simple, so I stuck with exactly what it is, and the good news is, it's not for grown ups. Nope, a life inventory is what 'growing ups' do, and that, gorgeous girl, is what we are, gorgeous growing ups. Being a grown up would suggest that we'd done all our learning and have all the information we could ever possibly need to take on the world, and I don't know about you, but that's definitely NOT me, not one little bit. So come on, let's do this thing.

Take a look at your life right now, write down each area of your life, for example; career, relationships, family, body, finances, love – feel free to be more specific – and write 'career' on one sheet, 'relationship' on another, and keep going until each heading has it's own piece of paper.

Mark yourself out of 10 for how you feel you're doing in that area right now. Then, and this may take some time, start to 'fess up. Remember, the important thing is to be honest and make NO judgments about yourself, okay?

Ask yourself the following questions:

- What feels good about this area of my life right now?
- What's not working in this area right now?
- Why? - This one may take some digging, but go there and keep going there, until you start to make some connections – just write it in a matter-of-fact style, without attachment. For example, if you're working on your finances and you're currently £45,000 in debt, simply write down why:

Because I've spent too much on my credit card.
Then ask the same question, why?
Because I wanted a pair of Vivienne Westwood heels.
Why?
Because I wanted something beautiful in my life.
Why?
Because I don't feel beautiful and shoes make me feel better.

Bingo – there's your answer.

Now, without judgement, ask yourself:

What score would I like this section to have this time next year?
   And what about 3 years time?
   What actions am I going to take to make that happen?

Try not to spend too much time on each one, but be as thorough and as honest as possible. There's no point lying, or trying to justify your reasons, the important part of taking a life inventory is the facts.

Once you've filled in all the blanks, it's time to make connections and join the dots. Maybe on your 'body' page you've written 'low self-esteem' which would then correlate with the fact you've got yourself in debt to buy shoes that make you feel better.

Now, write down the connections and see them unfolding in front of you – it might not feel 100% awesome, but being honest with yourself about where you're at now and why, will give you all the information you need to take the next step.

What is the next step?

Action, baby.

For example, on your 'finances' action list you might put:

'ring up 3 creditors and sort out a payment plan that works for me, paying off £15 a month, with a view to review it in 6 month time.'

Life rewards action. I can't say that enough, and when you're taking a step every day, no matter how small, in the direction of your destiny, you'll feel lighter and brighter, you'll be sending out feel-good vibes and you'll send a message to the universe that screams *'damn it dude, I mean business!'* The goodness that will start rolling your way when you act on a daily basis, from a place of truth and honesty – no masks, no pretence – will blow your mind, you wait and see!

DARING DAME: Sarah Prout

Sarah Prout is a bestselling author who writes about love, the universe and entrepreneurial sparkle. She was at the front of the queue when they were giving out anti-bullshit pills and I adore her honesty. She's selfless with in the way she shares what works and I love her for showing me how to have big adventures in manifesting – she'll show you too, she's ever-so good like that.

Sarah, Prout – who are you, gorgeous girl and what do you do?
I'm a writer with a brain and heart wired for creativity. I love to teach people how to live vibrant and creative lives based on what they are passionate about.

I've been fortunate enough to work with hundreds of fabulous businesswomen from around the globe. It's been such a thrilling ride connecting with highly inspired and like-minded clients that make it a true pleasure to work in the industry of personal development and business coaching.

One of the reasons you inspire me most is your ability to manifest awesomeness – how did you discover manifesting and its power, and how do you actually 'make it happen?'
I started studying meditation when I was 19. This was when I really started to explore spirituality and the connection it has to the results we are achieving in our lives. One of the most common threads explored in most spiritual texts and personal development books is GRATITUDE. This is the most potent juice in the manifesting process and in the entire Universe! If you feel thankful for the stuff in your life then more will just magically appear.

You are the Queen o' social media and your book, Power of Influence shows us how we can make it work for us – what impact can using SM correctly have on a new business?
Social media is the way we can connect to our audience and allow/invite them to get to know us a little better. The new currency of marketing is connection and engagement, so if you understand these two vital elements it will cause major ripples of success in the results you are getting fro your business.

You are kick-ass at brand development – why is branding so
ortant?
ling represents the message you are trying to convey about

your business message. You need to make sure it's an accurate representation of your mission. This can be such a creative and rewarding process to develop.

You're a mumma and an entrepreneur – how do you juggle the two? How do you find a balance?

Flexibility is the key to balancing parenthood and business pursuits. There are days that I plan and then go in completely the opposite direction. Multi-tasking and staying reasonably organized is an excellent goal to work towards.

What do you love most about being a woman in the world?

I have two answers to that question.

1. I truly believe that the soul has full male/female integration and that balance is essential as we live as spiritual beings having a physical experience on Earth.
2. Waterproof mascara, sexy knickers, lip-gloss, heels, anything fuchsia-hued and the cool way that we can grow babies in our bodies if we want to.

Who and what makes you happy, excites you, inspires you?

There are so many things that I choose to have in my life that I feel happiness about. My children and my boyfriend Sean make me happy. They fill my life with so much LOVE.

I also get excited about everything, especially if I've had too much coffee or sugar. I get inspired by people that are doing powerful things that impact the lives of others in the world. Authenticity is a real turn on and when I see people 'walking the talk' it's pretty thrilling.

What's a day in the life of Sarah like?

My days are generally very spontaneous. There are four things that I do each day consistently that I build my business/fun activities around…

- Meditation within the first half an hour of waking up
- Brainwave entrainment for 40 mins at around 4pm each day
- 100% Vegan diet
- Affirmations at night

How does your spirituality impact on your creativity?
Spirituality impacts everything, especially creativity! If I'm consistent with my meditations, affirmations and being healthy in general, then I find that my level of creative drive is consistently intense.

What has been your most magickal moment?
There are so many to choose from! I loved how my son wrapped his entire hand around my little finger within the first five minutes of being born. I loved finding out from a 3D scan that I was having a daughter. I loved running through cherry blossom trees as a kid in bare feet. I loved seeing a giant rainbow on the day I met my boyfriend. I tell you, any moment can be framed as your most magickal.

The key is to immerse yourself in the feeling of gratitude during every moment.

What must-have traits would we need for creating a career we love?
Inspiration, motivation and lashings of love: that's pretty much all you need.

What's the best advice you've ever been given?
Rinse the forks before they go in the dishwasher OR be careful what you wish for.

You're a creatrix of awesomeness – what advice can you impart on lady-kind?
Be independent and empowered enough to always seek happiness and validation within yourself. I'm one of those women that spent way too much time looking to the man in my life to feel truly alive. As ladies, we must always and only live for ourselves. Self-love is a gift you must allow in your life until the day the lights go out.

What's your life motto?
Live life with love and gratitude in every moment.

You want to make her your best friend too, don't you? Go find out more about her and her books by visiting her at: **www.sarah prout.com** - tell her Lisa sent you!

SENSUAL

"...To be sensual, I think, is to respect and rejoice in the force of life, of life itself, and to be present in all that one does, from the effort of loving to the making of bread..."
James A, Baldwin

Big time sensuality

Now, I don't know about you, but BS (Before SASSY), *way* before in fact, when I heard the term 'sensuality', I would think of all things sexy and ohh-la-la. You know, dimmed lights, sweet-smelling candles, silk sheets, and a li'l Marvin Gaye timed strategically to kick in the minute you *'get it on'* just like in the movies. Then I read copious amount of Anais Nin and realised that all things ohh la la, are never accompanied by Marvin Gaye. Ever. That's the stuff of a Hollywood schmaltz, but what about sensuality? What's that all about?

It's about juicy, delicious desires, unlocking your pleasure centre – knowing what it is and positively demanding it as often as possible, living a life of complete and utter joy and love stuff, being ecstatically happy, having an outrageously hot sex life, loving your bare behind, knowing what makes you come, asking for what you want both in and out o' bed, passionate living and loving, living a playful life – actually, it's a million things.

When I split from an eight-year relationship, I felt oppressed. I spent a lot of that relationship 'settling' and doing what I thought was expected, which is why, when it came to an end, I had two options.

1. Fall into the role of victim, beating myself about my inadequacies – in life, love, the universe and everything or 2. Make like goddess Akilhanda, and use the broken-ness of the relationship to create a new me and switch up my relationship behaviours. So, when I returned home from Paris after *that* New Year, I decided

to make like a Parisian, and take lovers. Now don't get your frilly tangas in a twist, it was hardly the stuff of an Anais Nin diary, but for the first time, in a long time, I was calling the shots and I'm not going to lie, I really rather liked it. I didn't fake orgasms, I didn't pretend to like something just to 'get it over with', and instead, I learned what I DID like and asked for more of it. LOTS more. It was incredibly liberating, but shhh, don't tell anyone because I'd HATE to ruin my reputation as a Francais Fancy Floozy, but it turns out I wasn't entirely cut out for lover-keeping, and my Parisian-inspired frissons lasted for the grand total of six months, but still, a girl can learn a LOT in six months.

Pursuing Pleasure
Now you don't need to take lovers in order to know what you want in the bedroom, or in life for that matter, but if you feel called, definitely give it a go, what you DO need to do, is spend time getting to know what it is you want. What you really, really want. Knowing what rocked my world in the boudoir was life-altering for me as it made me step up my pleasure quota in other areas of my life, and pleasure is what sensuality is ALL about.

We're not taught pleasure, we're not encouraged at any point to find out what makes us hot, what makes us smile, what makes us laugh out loud, but pleasure is an absolute SASSY super-power, because when you know that dancing in the rain, having your feet rubbed, listening to a certain song, being touched in a certain way, getting lost in a deep meditation, wearing come-to-bed lingerie under your work clothes, painting, flicks your pleasure switch, you can start to make sure there's a whole lot more of it in your life, and when there's more pleasure in your life? Days are brighter, people are nicer, dreams are easier to achieve and you, g-friend, vibe at a whole new insanely attractive level.

Miss Sensuality

Being, feeling, living, breathing, and experiencing yourself as a sensual being doesn't mean that you'll take to the stage and swing your nipple tassels – unless you want to, or that you'll make out with the entire local rugby team – unless you want to, or that you'll turn into a rubber-clad dominatrix – unless you want to, nope, being sensual is about you being ALL of your true self and that includes all of your desires, pleasures and fantasies, knowing what you like and dislike, and not being afraid to vocalise that in, and out of, the bedroom.

Ask yourself the following:

What is sensual?

Write down the first thoughts that come into your head. Don't analyse them, just write them down. It could simply be a picture in your mind, or a feeling in your body. Be aware of where in your body that feeling is and how it makes you feel.

What are you experiencing?

Is it that you're more sexy, more confident, more empowered, that you feel feminine, softer, funnier? Are you making different choices and decisions in your life? Are you steering your life in the direction you want to go? What does it look like? How does it feel? What thoughts and beliefs do you have? How does your body feel?

Maybe sensual is about pampering yourself more. Maybe you'd like to wear 1940s tea dresses, learn to Charleston or wear high-heels. Perhaps you'd like more self-confidence?

How do you act?

How does the sensual 'you' dress? How does the sensual 'you' take care of her body? Does the sensual 'you' exercise? What does the sensual 'you' eat? What does the sensual 'you' do for fun?

If you were asked to name a woman who represents the epitome of sensuality to you who would that be?

What is it about them that represents 'sensuality' to you?

Remember, this is all about YOU. There's no right or wrong about this exercise, and none of it's set in stone. As a SASSY super-hero-girl you're constantly changing and evolving, so you're likely to discover that the responses you have now change on your path to destination Destiny.

What do you feel you don't have in order to live life as a sensual, confident, feminine woman?

Keep going until you feel you've exhausted your list.

Now as you go about your life for the next few days, simply observe whether the beliefs you have about YOU and your sensuality are true. Start to notice how you're feeling having 'outed' all this information about yourself.

Simply observe yourself and really use all your senses to figure out what sensual means to you.

What's your pleasure?

"...An inordinate passion for pleasure is the secret of remaining young..."
Oscar Wilde

So are you in on the pleasure? This isn't an instant to-do task, you'll find that pleasure-seeking is a life long adventure, but, and this is super-important, it HAS to be a priority, something that you tend to, and nurture on a daily basis. Start by making a list of the things you KNOW bring you pleasure, then every day, make a note of the things that have brought you pleasure that day – what made you feel good? What made your belly flip? What gave you goosebumps of excitement? If you can't think of anything, you need to become a pleasure seeker, and then start following through on any, or all of the activities that can add to your own enjoyment and satisfaction.

Now before you start to find a gazillion reasons why you couldn't possibly do this, or you begin to tell yourself how selfish, or self-indulgent it would be to put yourself before your never-ending to-do list/your children/your partner – delete as applicable – this is an essential SASSY must-do. If you don't honour your pleasure, everything, and everyone, in your life will pay for it. I know it may feel naughty or wrong to acknowledge that you're putting yourself first, (it's not, btw,) but think of it this way; a mother must eat good food to produce good milk for her baby, right? There are no shortcuts there. It's just the facts. So be a good mother to everything, and everyone, in your life – family, colleagues, creative projects – by taking maximo care of your pleasure first.

You won't look back on this lifetime and be thankful for all the hours you worked at a job you hate, all the years you spent in a relationship that was tearing you apart inside, all the boring snoring hours you spent munching crisps and watching soap operas on the teev, the moments you'll look back on with a smile on your face and butterflies in your belly will be the beautiful, heart-pounding risks and rewards of total and utter pleasure. I make sure I live a life that's completely tuned in and turned on, and so should you!

Repeat after me: *I deserve pleasure!*

"If you don't love yourself, you cannot love others. You will not be able to love others. If you have no compassion for yourself then you are not able of developing compassion for others."
Dalai Lama

Now, when you meet another super-hero-girl o' SASSY who is in the process of discovering her super-hero-girl powers, I bet one of the first things you'll discover is that, at some point, she'll have given herself a hard time, not shown herself maximo love stuff, or tried to deal with her feelings with abusive and not-nice substances or activities. Whether it's food, shopping, drugs, alcohol, relationships or some other unhealthy behaviour, it's not until we know how to truly love ourselves up and fully embrace our powers o' SASSY, that we realise how uber-important self-care is to becoming the mistress o' our destiny. I get it though, sometimes you forget to put yourself first. Your goals, your responsibilities, your to-do list and well, real-life stuff gets in the way, doesn't it?

Except, these are just excuses.

Yes, modern living makes for busy girls, and yep, random stressy surprises WILL always pop up in life, but there really is NOTHING more important than providing yourself with huge amounts of life nourishment, filling up on acts o' totally delicious pleasure and falling crazy in crush with your beautiful self, because if you don't, that's when you start to stifle your dreams, creativity and intuition with not-niceness – in my case it was a vat of chocolate – in order to get a quick fix of the warm happy stuff, and yep, I won't lie, it worked for a little while, but long term, all you're really doing is drowning out the ancient call from the goddess girls that went before. Who, through your thoughts and dreams and feelings, are trying to desperately re-connect you to your kick-ass super-hero-girl powers of SASSY, the powers that are only truly unleashed when you show yourself the big love.

"Learning to love yourself is the greatest love of all."
Whitney Houston

I never need an excuse to belt out a Whitney classic, but if I did, this would most definitely be it. We love nothing more than to spread the love amongst our family and g-friends, to pay them compliments when they're talking trash about themselves, to buy flowers for them when they're sad, to give them time out when they're tired and need to rest, but when it comes to loving ourselves? Not so much.

The way I see it, loving your gorgeous self – and you are gorgeous, you know – should involve treating yourself the way you would treat your very best gal pal. I've got the most beautiful besties, and they won't mind me telling you that, like me, they're *far* from perfect, but I simply love and adore them nonetheless. In fact, I think they're pretty freakin' amazing. They're star-shaped girls who make my life better in a gazillion different ways simply by being in it. Which is why I have sat myself on exactly the same sparkly pedestal that I've perched those gorgeous girls on.

Why? Because if I don't give myself the same amount of love stuff that I give those girls, then you'd know about it. You'd see it in my posture, the way that I act, you'd sense it, and you'd feel it in my vibration. It would not be nice, I assure you. When you love yourself, life is better. It really is as simple as that.

Y'see, when you're not showing yourself the love stuff, the first place you'll notice it is physically. Your body is a tuning fork for awesomeness, and if it isn't being looked after and given all the goodness it needs, like fulfilling your life purpose, regular doses of complete and utter pleasure, it'll vibrate at a super-low frequency, and won't be able to pick up all the goodness that should be constantly flowing your way. When you ignore your dreams, or forget to give thanks for all the amazing things that are in your world, your kidneys have to work overtime to deal with the messy, stressy aftermath of a huge pizza binge, or the ibuprofen you've been taking to get rid of the icky headache you've got because you're stressing about a job you hate. You get the idea, right? Your system becomes overtaxed, it throws your hormones off balance and your energy levels are set to go-slow. These symptoms are a neon sign that your body is out of tune and desperately wants some love.

When your body's out of whack, *you're* out of whack. It's that simple. Which is sad, because you'll just not have the energy or the stamina to even begin to tap into your Spirituality, your Authenticity, your Sensuality or your ability to be truly Sensational and that is just wrong x 1000. Without showing yourself some serious self-love, you'll feel unfulfilled and incapable of reaching a place of true SASSYdom. Sure, it might sound a li'l woo-woo, but it's in that spirituality where you truly find your most kick-ass self. And, until you balance out the levels beneath it – physical, emotional, mental – you'll never be truly SASS-filled and able to become the mistress o' your destiny.

Y'see, you can tap into your super powers o' SASSY with the click of a manicured finger. You can call on the ancient goddess girls and wise women of the past for their intuitive knowledge, and use it to increase your own spiritual vibration and frequency for the good of all, not to mention, attract all of the money you want, live a fabulous life and manifest your soul mate too, which is never a bad thing, right? When your physical body is out of balance, it's like sending a message to the universe that you can't handle what you've got right now and you're definitely not ready for more. Creating a balance between your physical, emotional and spiritual self is quite possibly the best way to show yourself love, and when you do, you'll be sending nothing but love stuff right back out into the universe which, FYI, is one of the most powerful super-hero-girl tools of SASSY that there is – it's a win-win love fest!

> *"…Love yourself first and everything else falls into line. You really have to love yourself to get anything done in this world…"*
> **Lucille Ball**

Falling in love with your naked bee-hind is the most delicious gift you can give yourself, but it's not easy to show yourself the big naked love when you've been conditioned by society, the media, the porn industry to look and be a certain way. The simple answer, and the one you'll read in all the self-help books, is to love yourself, no matter what your shape or size. Except having had a somewhat tempestuous relationship with my own body, I know it's so much easier said than done. My body and I have not always had a love thing going on, far from it, but when I started to understand that real pleasure involved being nice to myself, and not treating my body as a trash can (just so you know, eating an entire family sized bar of chocolate in one sitting is *not* a pleasure you can't measure, it's a big, fat 'I'm-not-happy' clue) I worked on ways that would make me like myself a little more. And while I'm all about falling head-over-heels in crazy love on a first date, I totally understand that where your body's concerned, you may need to go on a few dates with yourself first, get to know each other before committing to the big lust-y, sensual love stuff. That's cool, you've got a life time to hang out, but if I were you, I'd start making out with yourself pretty soon, you don't want to miss out on all the lush, sensual, passionate flirtations and adventures you could have together do you?!

Real-girl yoga

Guess what? I heart yoga. Yep, one of my delicious ways to indulge in my own personal pleasure is to indulge in yoga.

Seriously, I never thought those words would *ever* leave my lips. I dance; I've dabbled in Pilates, but yoga? No, that really wasn't for the likes of me. I'm a size 18, I'm not a fan o' lycra and there is nothing even remotely ethereal or om-like about me.

Turns out I was totally wrong – and I am REALLY okay about being proven wrong – because after my first yoga class, it felt amazing. *I* felt amazing.

I was under the impression that yoga people were long, thin and bendy and really rather glorious. I am not, so I kept my distance from all things bendy-wendy. I'd often walk past the yoga class at the gym and drool a li'l bit at the girls who were doing it. I'd just pounded the treadmill (it's the exercise o' choice for big girls who go to the gym) and these girls looked all stretchy and positively serene.

I figured when I'd dropped a few dress sizes, I'd join in. But do you know what? It doesn't matter. Really it doesn't. Flexibility and strength have nothing to do with size. Your size, age and strength levels are irrelevant because the poses can be done with the level of intensity that suits you. Your practice can be adapted to your own limitations of time and space – see? Really it's the perfect-o form of exercise.

So I did it the SASSY way.

I did me some real-girl yoga.

I kicked the sofa back with two of my besties, and we did yoga together.

My body moved in deliciously different ways, I opened up my hips – my beau was all kinds o' happy about that – I stretched, I breathed and I stretched some more. I can't pretend that the first time I did it was beautiful and serene, mainly because there were lots of giggling, a variety of expletives that would make a sailor blush as our bodies experiences positions they'd never found themselves in – well, not whilst sober anyway – and I was petrified that I would fart. A lot. But, despite that, I found real love stuff for how it made me feel as a girl in the world.

Why does yoga rock for real girls?

It's a yummy way to move your body, especially if you haven't moved it a whole lot. If you carry extra weight, you limit your movements and yoga is a wonderful way to start moving again. As you begin to move your body, you find yourself able to cultivate a li'l grace as you improve your sense of balance, and lengthen and strengthen the muscles.

When you do the yoga poses, you develop an intimate relationship with your own body: you become aware of muscles you didn't know you had, aware of how much longer, looser and taller you can feel, and aware that your body is pretty freakin' amazing and able to move in ways you just didn't think were actually possible. Now this really matters because awareness of your body is the first step to acceptance of your body – and what member o' lady-kind doesn't want that?

Yoga. A delicious pleasure. One of my favourite things. And FYI, if you think yoga is an easy option in comparison to a pounding on the cross trainer, think again. I sweat like a bee-atch and feel every single muscle the next day. Yoga, the exercise o' real girls!

Snake hips and nipple-tassels

Crushing on my body became a whole lot easier when I found my quirks and worked them. Discovering your unique selling points, the things that make you gorgeously authentically you, is yet another key to unlocking your super-girl SASSY powers. My quirks include being a retro loving member o' lady-kind who hearts French cinema, always has a colouring book and felt tip pens to hand as a form of meditation, dresses like a 1950s housewife, bakes cupcakes in heels, has an intense knowledge of 1990s boy bands, and taps into all things yummy and sensual through belly dance and burlesque.

While I may not have ever wanted to be a rock-girl thrashing out a three chord tune on stage in front of a crowd of millions, my rather deliciously fabulous ways to really connect with my own super-hero-girl powers of sensuality is to indulge in the very old, and very popular forms of entertainment, Burlesque and belly dance. My big dream is to combine the two in a vaudeville style performance and take to the stage at the Crazy Horse in Paris – step aside, Miss Von Teese!

Belly dancing

Oh belly dancing, how I heart thee.

I discovered my love of all things belly dance when I took a five-week taster course at The Art House in Southampton. teacher, Akasha, a kick-ass German lady who specialises Tribal Fusion belly dancing, ignited a passion in me that burns crazy-bright.

Many experts say belly dancing is the oldest form of dance, having its roots in all ancient cultures from the orient to India to the mid-East. Probably the greatest misconception about belly dancing is that it is intended to entertain boykind. Not even. While I'm sure they definitely enjoy it, throughout history, this ritualised expression has usually been performed for other women, generally during fertility rites or parties preparing a young woman for marriage. In most cases, the presence of men is not permitted.

One of the many, many reasons I love belly dancing is because it's natural to a woman's bone and muscle structure with movements originating from the torso rather than in the legs and feet. The dance often focuses on isolating different parts of the body, moving them independently in sensuous patterns, weaving together the entire feminine form. Not only does it look beautiful, it's a super-hot way to emphasise the intimate physical connection between the dancer, her expression, and Mumma Earth – what's not to love about that?

There are hundreds of belly dance variations; my preferred choice is the slightly edgier don't-mess-with-me-wildness of Tribal Fusion. It has touches of flamenco anger, Native Indian pride and body popping energy, and is some way from the curvaceous, sequined femininity of traditional Egyptian styles. The costumes are less floaty and more folkloric/gypsy-inspired, a lot of the girls rock killer inkage and the moves aren't choreographed, instead, participants learn a common vocabulary of movement, and through subtle cueing and a lot of practice to develop non-verbal communication, dancers can create a performance that appears choreographed to the audience. Vocabularies vary from tribe to tribe, much like a regional language or slang, ndividual moves or short combos – it's freakin'

.-o-girl in all things tribal belly dance is Rachel
ou Tube her now, she wears an armoury of tusks and
..gs, has a thorny tattoo winding up and over one hip and
when she dances, the effect is quite terrifying and devastatingly
sexy. HAWT.

Burlesque – Burlesque began in the 1840s and was used by the
working class performers as a way to mock the upper classes,
their traditions, social habits, culture and fashion and many of
the performances were spoofs of operas, Shakespeare and other
classic literature and plays.

Today Burlesque is hot, hot, hot and encourages you to
embrace your sexuality, your femininity and be completely
confident in expressing yourself in a truly SASSY way – hurrah!

The beauty of burlesque is that it's for everyone, in that it
doesn't depend on performers being a certain size, shape or
fitness level – it's more about grace, posture and the magick you
create with your audience. Props are important too and give the
performer something to work with. These range from a simple
chair to something as elaborate as Dita von Teese's giant martini
glasses or Catherine D'Lish's birdcage. Some performers even
take it a stage further and include 'novelties' such as axe
throwing and fire breathing – but I don't recommend you try this
at home!

Gypsy Starfire
Meet Gypsy Starfire, my burly-girl alter-ego. She's SASSY, obv.,
and conjures up magick with just the twinkle of an eye.

I have a li'l bit of a girl crush on her, mainly because she takes
to the stage in a sparkly bra and corset combo, and shakes her
frilly knicker-ed behind with her gorgeous Art in Motion gal-
pals. Something I, as Lisa Clark would NEVER, EVER have

dreamed of doing. When I signed up to burlesque classes, it was to learn to dance, to find new ways to move and accept my body and to have fun, all of which we do in big, beautiful abundance, but the idea of actually performing in front of people? That was NOT on my list of things to-do. Well, it turns out this list-loving lady was about to go off list because... well, it's so much freakin' fun!

Ms Starfire is a super-hero version of me. She is totally confident and self-assured, rocks false eyelashes and fishnets and can move seductively in pretty ensembles. She is now my total go-to girl when I need to rock a presentation or if I feel belly nerves before delivering a workshop to over 100 girls – don't fret, I won't be shaking my tail feathers in nothing but a pair of frilly knickers, but now, in any situ of nerves, fear and scary-ness, I ask myself, *What Would Starfire do?*

Why?

Because I KNOW the answer, whatever the question, will be: kick some ass, g-friend!

Why don't you do the same? You don't have to go s'far as to actually perform on stage, although I absolutely, positively recommend it – it's the biggest most exciting buzz, I'm hooked! – but if you don't feel filled-to-the-brim with star-girl confidence, think about the girl you *would* be if you *did* have that confidence – what is she like? How does she act? What would she wear? I'm guessing she's pretty darn fabulous, right?

So today, imagine that you're her.

Give her a name.

Start being as happy/vampy/confident as she is, start walking tall, smile, think in the same way as she'd think, develop a twinkle in your eye.

What you put out there g-friends, will bounce right back at'cha. If you walk around with a gloomy face, moaning about how unfair life is – people will feel drained when they're around you and will avoid you at all costs.

Instead, beam out fabulousness, beam out smiles, beam out compliments and pink glitter-filled thoughts – it'll come back to you x 100. Promise!

Daring Dame: Immodesty Blaize
If you really want to know what burlesque is, you absolutely, positively need to watch Immodesty Blaize perform. I could not adore a woman more. Yep, I have a girl-crush. For sure, she has smouldering charm and larger-than life stage presence, but she's intelligent, articulate, warm and funny too. This international showgirl superstar, novelist, and undisputed queen of modern burlesque, is SASSY personified wrapped in a beautifully curvy, corseted package. Yes, I'm gushing. So, without further ado, I present to you, the beyond beautiful Miss Immodesty Blaize.

For the uninitiated, can you describe burlesque, and tell us about how you became a burlesque performer?
It's an historic form of erotic and ironic cabaret; funny men, sexy women, and above all, entertainment. It's been around for hundreds of years.

It appears in the French lexicon – *burlesque* – `meaning derisive imitation or grotesque parody, the older Italian and spanish – *burlesco* or *burla* – meaning both jest or joke, and the Latin term – *burra* – meaning trifle or nonsense. Burlesque has had many performance styles over the centuries, from Ancient Greek musical comedies, to 19th century satirical theatre, to 1940s blue comics to 1960s Vegas bump 'n' grind. One thing all burlesque styles share is the presence of some form of wit and erotica, whether it's a comic sketch, a bawdy lampoon, or a striptease. The striptease element of a burlesque show is a recent American development, which happened in the last 70 years, popularised by impresarios such as the Minsky brothers. The burlesque style I perform is based on the classic American striptease tradition of 20th century. When I started performing burlesque twelve years ago there were no burlesque clubs, or a scene, or any mainstream cultural awareness of the genre. I had to preach to the unconverted for many years about this genre but after working with Goldfrapp in 2002, I noticed the mainstream audience and press began to sit up and listen.

How would you describe your performance style, because let's face it, Miss Immodesty, you are NOT a cheesecake-kinda girl!
Maybe the lovechild of Anita Ekberg and Sophia Loren under a shower of Liberace's rhinestones being sprinkled by Wonderwoman? I have a passionate character that derives from my European roots so I can't keep the va-va-voom out of my performances. That's why tutus and fluff don't suit me!

There's something very magickal about watching you work your charm on stage – can that 'confidence and charm' be taught or is that passion and fire intrinsically part of who you are as a woman?
For this genre you need something of yourself on stage, it's a very personal expression. I happen to be a passionate person. I believe your style and persona has to come from the heart for it to be consistent and convincing. Confidence is just something that you can discipline yourself to have. It's not unusual for performers to be naturally shy or reserved when not on stage, that sensitivity is what allows us to be inspired and see things other people don't. But we must come out of ourselves – or I should say, be our true, unreserved selves on stage because if we want to express something then it's not an option to be shy. There's often that paradox with performers.

Do you see burlesque as an example of women reclaiming their own sexuality?
I am an entertainer, so my priority is to entertain my audience. I certainly don't perform as a means to resolving any personal

feminist issues I may have! I happen to think we've been free to own and express our sexuality openly in the Western world in a variety of ways for quite some time now, so I don't feel like we have anything left to reclaim necessarily, I think we already have pretty much every option available to us! If anything I quite enjoy reintroducing the idea of allure and mystique; keeping something back. Glamour is a spell, quite simply. In order to cast that spell you have to entice or mesmerise the audience with something. Part of that involves denying them access to absolutely everything, or puncturing the bubble with anything 'everyday'. But that applies to other genres and media too.

What do you love most about being a woman in the world?
I value the rights we have today, and I enjoy that I'm able to run a business without having to succumb to social pressures of marriage and children, or having to suffer bigots; but it's not a worldwide luxury, and my job is a constant reminder that I am truly lucky to be able to express my art in many places with freedom. We still have such a long way to go in many social and geographical cultures to move anywhere near gender equality or even just basic respect.

You've said that your 'hourglass figure' was not on-trend when you were growing up. Do you think a more voluptuous figure is truly any more acceptable in the mainstream today? If so, do you think part of burlesque's popularity is because of this celebration of a woman's curves?
I think there is a whole industry devoted to scrutinizing and criticizing women's appearances, in the form of blogs, celeb magazines etc. so I don't think any figure is particularly accepted – it's a *damned if you do, damned if you don't* kind of culture right now. Realistically the fashion industry will always continue to depict very thin women, it's how they believe their clothes look best; and mainstream media will continue to bitch and snipe and

pick holes in women's appearances for pretty much anything – evidently that must be what we like to read – what does that say about us? I'd like to think that the size zero debate of the last decade has brought the importance of health and sanity over dress size into the open. But then the media undoes all that work by constantly using the word 'curvy' as a euphemism for 'fat' so that anyone with any kind of shape left or right of an ironing board is now somehow 'fat'. Ultimately I think it would be healthy for the media to stop talking about what looks right or wrong, and consider that we are not all the same, we aren't meant to look the same, and we don't all like the same things, and that's really okay!

What attracted me to the genre of burlesque was the fact that it promotes the idea of individuality, and personality. Not just in appearance, but that the biggest stars got where they were by being memorable – and for that, they had to be different. They had a persona, a character; they had their own gimmick, their own visual identity, their own brand. Rather than the celeb culture today in which we're all encouraged to aspire to be like someone else, or to *fit in* or be *on trend*. Why would we want to look like someone else or follow a trend like sheep? Are we really that unimaginative? Burlesque flies in the face of that, and any serious performer is all about being themselves. You do see more womanly body shapes in the genre than I think you do in film or fashion, and I think that is partly because burlesque striptease had its golden age in the 50s when women did have a typically curvaceous hourglass shape, and there is a trend for recreating that aesthetic - but that isn't the only body type in burlesque today. It's not just about celebrating curves or shape, it's about celebrating the individual.

Have you always had a go-for-it-girl attitude?
I just like trying new things. I didn't want to follow anyone else's path. I was academic at school so I guess there was something

rebellious in me that wanted to do something unconventional just to piss people off, I don't know if it was the strict Catholic school upbringing or a mother who went to the Joan Crawford school of charm, who knows. I had no idea what I was doing in terms of building a business when I started out as there was no-one doing the same thing, no blueprint to follow. I had to just go for it. I learnt that mistakes are not mistakes, they are just lessons that help the end product. I started out in film when I left university, and I definitely never set out to be a performer – I had never been a stage school kid, yet subconsciously I created a job that fulfilled all the creative things I loved to do in one go – the writing, the designing, the movement, the visual, the music, the travel. Sure it's a risk to be unconventional, but you can make a much bigger picture if you have the balls to colour outside the lines!

You're a girl o' many, many talents, is it hard carving a career in this business they call 'show' and what do you think is the secret to your success?
Firstly the business of show is full of other people's glittery ideas about what is success; but it's a personal thing – I think it's important to go in with your own clear goals and be honest about what's important to you, and not be sucked into other people's ambitions or be limited by other people's expectations. Carving any kind of career in show is always going to take dedication and commitment. I have had to be disciplined about juggling priorities when I'm working across several media simultaneously – writing, developing or designing material or products takes time, yet the public don't see that side. They only see the end product, and especially these days they expect a different album or show every week from artistes – because that's how X-Factor churn it out. Don't be distracted, just keep going.

What's the best advice you've ever been given?
Accommodate, but never compromise.

What's your life motto?
Love conquers all.

**Can you tell us about the work that goes into a performance -
what inspires you, how does it go from an idea in your head to
a hugely camp, beauty*licious stage o' sparkle and delight?**
I can be inspired by anything; art, music, cinema, travel... the
very first wisp of an idea for the giant telephone act came from
Blondie's song 'Hangin on the Telephone' for example. I then
developed it as a 40s femme fatale act because in film noir the
telephone is a central plot device for intrigue – a murder plot, a
wiretap, an illicit affair, a sinister rendezvous, a fatal missed
call... I even used film noir film score to build the mood. And
then at the point where the giant 'phone rings, it all becomes
camp, frivolous and fabulous in the spirit of the old Italian 'white
telephone' movies. I don't expect everyone to look for my
reference points, so long as they enjoy the act – but they're there
if anyone is interested in the thought behind it. I design and
commission the props, also the costumes. I have to listen to my
music over and over and visualize the act, then write myself a
script for how the costume has to work and come off for certain
crescendos in the music. I'll make scrapbooks full of mood
boards, and I'll make loads of drawings, which I then take to my
costumiers and we figure out how to engineer everything from
headdress to heels, and we have numerous fittings until it all
works. I either work with composers or producers to edit
existing music or write new pieces. I have a fantastic team of
artisans who help me produce my vision, but I don't have stylists
telling me what to wear, or people manufacturing acts for me or
'borrowing' things from other performers' acts. It's my own
work.

What must-have traits would we need for stage-worthy confidence, presence and sexiness?

There's no mystery to confidence, it's just about self-knowledge, as without that, you cannot have self-acceptance. It's not about screaming for attention - the loudest people are not necessarily the most confident ones. Just spend some time allowing yourself to be human, to have flaws, and accepting some you can change, some you cannot, and you concentrate on making the best of your good points. In terms of sex appeal, the less you try the better. Your confidence is what gives you sex appeal! I think it's worth remembering the all-important tease too. As Sophia Loren said, *'sex appeal is 50% what you have, and 50% what people think you have'.*

To find out more about this gorgeous lady, check out her website: **www.immodestyblaize.com**

Lustful intentions

"...Does my sexiness upset you?
Does it come as a surprise
That I dance like I've got diamonds at the meeting of my thighs?..."
Maya Angelou, 'Still I Rise'

Now love stuff is good, yes? Self-love, the sweet and tender relationship kinda love, the warm and fuzzy love you feel for your best friends, your fam or a furry pet, but, how 'bout the lust-filled, sweet and tender, sensual stuff?

You've started dating yourself, you've discovered your quirks and how to work them, now how about falling in lust with yourself? Lust is all about the attraction, the desire, the allure, the yearning.

Look at yourself like you're a goddess who must be worshipped. Think Cleopatra, she was a total seductress and she started by seducing herself. She tended to her every need first. She listened to her desires and acted on them, bragged about her fabulosity, she created gorgeous sweet-smelling concoctions to wear because she was worth it. She let herself, and those around her, know just how important she was.

Channel your Cleopatra and today enter into a flirtatious frisson with yourself. Pay yourself compliments, wink at yourself in the mirror, and give your reflection a minx-y smile. Be kind to yourself, really listen to your body and feed it what it needs, does it want to be touched? Does it want to eat mangoes naked? It really is the only way to eat a mango.

Lusting after yourself is the perfect opportunity to see yourself as a lover might in all your gorgeous, amazing, seductive glory. Delight in yourself. Over and over. Feels good doesn't it?

Do it again.

Touch-y subject
Yep, let's go there.

Let's talk about masturbation. Touching yourself. Self-pleasure, bringing yourself off. Unless you fully know all about your vulva – how it works, what it looks like and how it makes you feel, you'll never be able to direct anyone else to your pleasure centre, and believe me they generally DO need direction. Is this convo making you feel uncomfortable? Boy-kind talk about bringing themselves off with ease, so why is it such a taboo for lady-kind? It's no surprise that we can't talk about 'getting it on' with ourselves when we usually refer to it as 'down there' in hushed tones. Our place of pleasure, our genitalia, our vulva, our clitoris, our vagina is the area that shall not be named, and by not naming it, we're basically saying it doesn't exist – how sad is that? This is the most beautiful jewel in the treasure box of a woman, yet the only names we can come up with are pussy, mini ha-ha, flu-flu and va-jay-jay. Personally, I use the Sanskrit term, *Yoni*, I think it sounds sensual and positively love-filled, don't you? If we don't name it something we love, how on earth are we going to show it love? And that is a real SASSY super-hero-girl power knowing that you have insta-access to pleasure at the flick (or touch, or rub, or stroke) of your pleasure switch. Your clitoris, your very own pleasure button, which literally has no other function except to give you delicious feel-good pleasure – seriously, if ever there was a reason to be a girl in the world, that's got to be it – is not to be ignored, it should be positively celebrated. So if you don't already, make a habit of making out with yourself. After a bath, in the shower, on clean crisp bed sheets, on a super-soft rug, while reading erotic fiction – use your fingers, use sex toys, rub, flick, stroke and play with yourself – find what works for you and get to know what makes your cheeks redden and your heart beat a li'l faster – do you like how it feels? Do it some more. It's the most delicious way to bust stress and make you smile; it's the perfect-o mood enhancer. In fact, maintaining a regular diet of delicious self-pleasuring will set your vibin' to a 'crazy attractive' level, so much so that if you already have a partner, they will deffo want in on the action, and if you don't, you will be sending out big *'I'm totally worthy and know what I want'* signals to attract the right kind of partner, you'll also have an awesome repertoire of yumm-o sensations that you can teach them once the woo-ing of you has commenced – hurrah.

FYI: Touching yourself, bringing yourself off, making out with your sweet self is not naughty or dirty, despite what you may have been brought up to believe – the more we discuss it, and the more we do it, the less of a taboo it will be, and the better sex we'll have – hurrah!

Sexual healing
Now, I'm no sexpert, and I'm deffo not about to write a chapter about *how* to have sex, I'll leave that to *Cosmo* magazine, but I do

actively encourage the act of sex wholeheartedly. The kind of sex that involves EVERY person involved feeling pleasure, delight and delicious feel-good yumminess. Sound too good to be true? It's not, it's totally doable and it's a beyond beautiful way to align your SASSY super powers – there is nothing NOT to love about SASSY sex, I promise.

One thing I know for sure, is that love = mind-blowing, magnificent sex. Sex does not necessarily create magnificent love. Sex without love can definitely be pleasurable, but for me, the healthiest, most delicious sex is preceded by intimacy: emotional sharing, appreciation, and spiritual connection.

Love is the answer. No matter what the question.

Don't just take my word for it, go try it out.

LOTS.

Don't have sex – what I mean is, spend some time in bed without having actual sex, simply touch and stroke and kiss each other. Enjoy each other. Intimacy rocks.

Stay connected – when we get excited sexually, we have a tendency to fall into our own pleasure-seeking experience, and while it's really important that your own needs are met, (really, it is, please make sure they are) the deepest ecstasy 'comes' from staying connected, rather than drifting into your own sensations and feelings. Maintain eye contact – tantra style – for a real intense connection.

Communicate – You can't expect your partner to read your mind, to know your needs, desires, feelings and thoughts if you don't tell them, and you'd be a fool to think you could, or should, second guess theirs either. For sex that will have you bouncing off the walls with pleasure, communicate. Don't be afraid to tell, or show, your partner what you like, sex is to be enjoyed, not endured. Ask your partner what turns them on – do they like it when you touch them there? How about here? If you want to try something new or different, don't just assume your partner will enjoy it, discuss it, make it a playful experience, being sure to lavish your partner with crazy love and appreciation when they hit the spot – we all like to know when a job's well done, right? Personally, I can't think of a better way to spend a day than taking the time to explore each other's pleasures. Hmmmm. Forget the gym, that's a workout I'll happily subscribe to – mind, body and soul.

Give AND receive - A lot of lady-kind give, give, give during sex to cover up the fact that we have issues receiving the good stuff. Not anymore, sweet thing. You are absolutely, positively worthy of love, pleasure and affection, know it, own it and most importantly, enjoy it.

The Big O – There's no right or wrong way to come, but the act of climax is pretty freakin' awesome. Some women may, at times, feel their orgasm all over the body, reverberating through their skin, while some may feel a more contained pulsing sensation between their labia – it doesn't matter where you feel it, what matters is that it feels good. So try out different positions, speeds and angles, battery – or mains-powered vibrations tend to give a more immediate orgasm with stronger contractions, but that doesn't mean you'll prefer the sensation to a slower build-up and a milder orgasm with your partner – you might like both, in different ways on different days – don't you just love being you?

Daring Dame: Sam Roddick

The first time I saw Sam Roddick on TV she had picked up a Double Pleasure dildo, stroked it rather affectionately, and stated in a very matter-of fact way that, *'it's absolutely brilliant for finding the g-spot.'* What is not to love about a woman who is so open, real, passionate and honest about sex? To give you an idea of the awesomeness that is Sam, she's the founder of *Coco de Mer*, a British 'erotic emporium' dedicated to the celebration of sexual pleasure, empowerment, dignity and discovery and her twitter profile reads: *Artistic pleasure provocateur, passionate activist, creative thinker, disobedient filthy mouthed feminist, celebrator of loving masculinity and feminine power.* Sam is my sexual heroine – so, lets talk about sex, baby!

I'm a girl o' the world, yet I still get crazy looks when I talk openly about pleasuring myself, having an orgasm, sexuality. How can we change this up and have a more open dialogue about this among lady-kind?
Well that is exactly my mission... to open up society and to promote a loving sense of ease around the truth about sex. The only way to promote being comfortable with the subject of sex is by doing what you're doing — being open, unashamed and above all being honest I have a question for you... do you honestly talk about masturbation techniques that you apply to yourself publicly? If so, you are the coolest person I know. Female masturbation is one of the biggest social taboos around and there are not many women willing to share their tips. It is for this reason that so many women are left in the cold when it comes to orgasms, so I fully support your masturbation mission and keep on talking.

What does true sexual liberation really mean?
The only way to really understand liberation is to fully embrace the concept and importance of consent. Once we understand that consent is not about a yes or a no, but a negotiation of what is truly on offer. It is about respecting people's personal choices. The only liberated sex is true consensual sex, beyond that... sex is a journey of self discovery and exploration

And how do you think we can start to reclaim our own sexuality?
By embracing your body, being curious about your emotions and challenging your intellect.

Can sex be used to heal ourselves?
YES, it is the most intimate and self-revealing and loving act you can engage in. I have definitely healed myself through exploring my relationship and responses to sex. Sex always leads us to our heart. How we love ourselves and how we love others is the most important aspect of our lives to discover grow and enrich.

SASSY encourages women to discover real magic in every day situations and that includes having great sex that fulfills, pleasures, excites and makes us happy – how important is the art o' pleasure and how can we expand our repertoire?
I think sex can add a huge amount to our personal happiness and our lives. After all, it is something that scientists have determined as a human need (which is something that we cannot live without).

Therefore, if we approach it, as it is a human need then we need to invest some great thinking/feeling/understanding /creativity into it. The most important thing to comprehend is that sex is not a function, it isn't something you do or have done to you, it is a physical, emotional expression, once you can start to be very creative about it.

I heart Rumi, you heart Rumi – how does he inspire your work?
Yes, Rumi is at the heart of all I do - ecstatic and passionate love – that embraces the spiritual while gets drunk on life. If you love Rumi, you will wet your knickers over Hafiz.

Your shop was THE sexiest shop I've EVER bee
share your reasons for making it your mission to
shops...

Because sex shops were not designed before I st
Mer. They were and mostly still are insult to senses and full of
toxic crap toys that would make you want to gag! They put
women off sex not turn them on. I wanted to create a sexual
aspiration, a place that transformed the way society and culture
related to sex to inject love, intimacy and pleasure into the world
of sex and sexuality. I wanted to create a world that reflected for
me the best aspects of sex – which is all about connectivity I
wanted it to be witty beautiful and luxurious.

I heart Anais Nin – how important do you think erotic liter-
ature for women in exploring their own sexuality?

Our brain is a sexual organ – Anais Nin is like reading lyrical
filth, she is delicate and yet brazen, she is soft and hard. She is a
contradiction between vulnerability and strength, she is a must
read on any woman's reading list.

Your sex toys are bee-you-tiful – what's your advice for buying
a sex toy?

Always remember, it's not the sex toy that brings you pleasure,
it's how you apply it! Sex toys are like a conductor's stick, they
creatively inspire variety in the bedroom – start simple, and then
progress!

What do you love most about being a woman?

I love being a woman, the emotions, motherhood and being a
receptor to life. I love having boobs as I find them so comforting
and I love my pussy as it has so many emotions attached to it and
for the immeasurable pleasure it has given me.

you tread your own path and make your own killer heel footprints — one of the many, many reasons I heart you, Miss Sam – what has encouraged this Go-girl attitude? Have you always had it?

We all have it – the difference was my mum and grandmother gave me total permission to be me – they also were women who stood up and out. I feel it is our time in history, so girls, women, feline seductresses, rise up and be unforgivably you!!! The world needs more brilliant and kick ass women to claim their space.

You're a girl o' many, many talents, has it been hard to carve a career in the sex industry, and what do you think is the secret to your success?

Passion, naivety and blind determination.

What's the best advice you've ever been given?

Enjoy the process!

What's your life motto?

Fuck it!

One of Sam's big concepts around sex is that, if, as a society we are more sexually satisfied, we'd be a trillion times happier and war wouldn't happen – she obviously expresses her thoughts far more eloquently than that, but you get the idea, right? Sexual satisfaction – consensual, ENJOYABLE, bed-rocking delicious sex = mucho happiness. Mucho happiness = no war. No war = peace and mahoooosive love stuff. Now I'm rubbish at maths but *those* equations rock my world – let's do it. Let's make out. LOTS.

SENSATIONAL

Are you sensational?

Do you arouse strong curiosity, interest, or a reaction? Being truly sensational is to stand out, stand tall, to wear a leopard-print lycra catsuit whilst doing the weekly shop, to put a crazy idea out in the world and have such blind determination that it will actually happen despite all the people that have told you it wouldn't. When you're sensational, your actions aren't necessarily to shock, although sometimes they might be and absolutely should be, you just follow the pleasure, listen to the heart song, play, learn and enjoy the ride.

Have you ever wondered why some girls just seem to totally rock n' rule at whatever they do? Like the girl who walks into a room and completely enchants everyone simply by being in it, or the girl who everything just seems to go absolutely right for, You know the girls I'm talking about, right?

I used to be envy-green of the girls who Lady Luck smiled upon, *'why them?'* I'd ask, *'why not me?'* except, I never actually listened to the reply. If I had of done, I'm absolutely positive the Goddess/divine would of hollered back: *'you make your own good fortune, sweet thing, now quit the pity party and go make beautiful, big miracles happen!'*

The good news is that when you're SASSY, you become one of those girls. In fact, I'll let you into a secret, you *are* one of those girls already; but to fully shine, like the star girl you absolutely, positively are, you have to discover four very important SASSY super-hero-girl powers – luck, good fortune, charisma and charm, (Clue: they're all inside you!) Learn as much as you can about them, then, and this is the fun bit, you work them bad boys as if your life depends on it, it doesn't, but your life will be a whole lot more bliss-kissed if you do!

Charm School

Charm is one of my all time favourite SASSY super-hero-girl powers, because it's not just a cute accessory for your handbag; it's a great way to cast a spell of absolute fabulosity over everyone you meet. All you need to start is an open mind and a willingness to lead an amazing life.

So many people laughed when I declared that I wanted to do something special in the world, they shot down my big beautiful thinking and signed me up for the impossible mission of proving that I could do as well as, or better than the entire population of boy-kind.

Enter SASSY-fication. A gentle nudge from the divine to remind us all that our power lies not in competing with boykind, but in fully embracing our womanly strengths – to love, to live big dreams, to be expressive, sensual, inspirational, to speak our truth, to be intelligent and compassionate, while rocking a slash of hot pink lipstick – to be the amazing, magickal beings that lady-kind were born to be.

Lesson one: Be prepared

Charming people always have something to talk about in *every* situation, so be prepared. Not in a false or forced way, but when you take a general interest in life and the lives of others, you'll always have something to say. I always carry or wear a conversation piece. It can be an interesting piece of jewellery, a cute bag that you've customised yourself, a pin badge with your favourite slogan or catch phrase – anything that will break the ice or prompt people to ask you about it. When they do, have a little story ready, *'Oh this scarf? Well, funny you should ask actually...'* don't, however, prepare and rehearse actual statements or jokes or you'll sound like an extra from a really, really bad daytime soap opera. Having an item that actively provokes conversation, gives you the opportunity to talk and interact with new people – I've actually found freelance work on a train based on the ridiculously oversized pink flower I was wearing in my hair. The lady across from me commented on my accessory of loveliness, we got talking, she was the ed-girl of a women's magazine, she commissioned me there and then – I can't promise you the same luck, but if you leave the house each day with the intention that good things are going to come your way, chances are they will!

Lesson two: Take and give compliments
Most mornings I wake up and I thank the gorgeous goddess for my ability to accessorise. I love to prettify my hair before I leave the house and always wear some form of oversized flower/headscarf/headband combo in it, I wear ridiculously over-the-top jewellery and have an uncountable amount of obscure shoes and handbags, as I mentioned above, at some point during the day, someone will react to these, and when they do, you have two options. You can blush bright pink, stumble on your words, make your excuses and scurry away, or you could smile a big smile and thank them for being so lovely – you see it's really rather rude not to accept a compliment, if someone takes time out to share their love of your ensemble or the way you wear your hair, or compliment something you have written or said, you need to be graceful and thankful. That way, that person will keep sharing the love in the future, and you get to collect compliments like they're yummy candy – hurrah!

Giving compliments is really rather fabulous too, but only give them if you mean them, they need to be from the heart, and not just because you feel you have to.

Lesson three: Make others feel important
We all want to be desired and feel like we matter, don't we? When you're charming you know how to make that happen. I've got a friend who is in a super-high powered job, yet she has the ability to recall names of people she's met long ago and even when the name escapes her, she remembers the encounter. She

knows how to make people feel important and everyone likes to feel important.

To make people feel comfy, you must first feel comfy in your own skin. Even if you're dishing out compliments and remembering names, if you're nervous and insecure, your attempted charming gestures will carry little weight. It's equally important that you can make people feel at ease around you. I went through a stage of having to mention to everyone I came into contact that I was from a council estate. I thought I'd make it clear from the outset otherwise there was a chance that they'd find out later and make judgements about me. Regardless of whether you're from a council estate or a country pile, don't be intimidated or critical of your background, or that of others. Connecting is not about status; it's about being able to relate to people from all walks of life – that's real charm.

Lesson four: Be Interesting
Sadly, the world is full of self-absorbed people who are needy, insecure and always seeking approval – none of these are entirely attractive qualities, but when you work your SASSY super-hero-girl charm, you know the power of taking the focus off of yourself and placing it on the other person. You don't walk into the room worried about what you look like, if people will like you or if you're going to say something stupid. You don't need approval, and you really don't care what people think about you. You want to know about others and your curiosity outside of your own li'l world makes you a rather charming rarity!

I don't want to disappoint you, but no one really cares about how big your pile o' bricks are, what kind of car you drive or how much money you make. However, what makes your heart sing, the last great book you read, an event you attended, or an experience you've had, now that g-friend, is interesting.

To be charming, you need to cultivate your own passions and knowledge base so that you can always add something interesting to the convo mix. For me, I'll know that if I talk about my love of retro movies, burlesque or belly dancing, I almost immediately capture their attention. If not, I also know about baking the perfect cupcake, how to accessorise ANY ensemble, and how to write a haiku. Diversity adds charm. Fact.

Lesson five: Get Lippy
Your smile is a definite VIP pass to popularity. It makes you appear friendly and enthusiastic and totally approachable. It has to be genuine though – you can't just paint a perma-grin on your face and expect people to fall for it. For pure SASSY magnetism, try the 'spill-over' smile. Look someone in the eyes, then, let a slow smile build up on your whole face as if in response to the genuine affection you're feeling towards them. It'll bag you a sincere smile – not a phoney, instant people-pleasing one.

Lesson six: Touching stuff
Physical contact can work wonders to maximise your bond with someone, whether it's your crush du jour or a potential boss. Whether it's a simple brush of your hand or a full-on hug, you'll send love-me waves surging through them. Watch their actions too – if they run their hands through their hair, mirror it. Mirroring happens naturally in social interactions, but when you're conscious of it and you're aware of its affects, it can be used as a tool in effective communication for generating rapport.

Next time you're engaged in a convo with someone, try mirroring body language, posture, and facial expressions. You will find that the conversation suddenly feels very friendly and open.

It's a sure-fire way to build affection. Make it subtle though, you don't want them to think you're mocking them.

Lesson seven: Hear-say
The single most important thing you can do to make people dig

you is easy – just listen to them! It's a huge compliment to have someone's total attention – gal pals will trust you with their deepest, darkest secrets and colleagues will be blown away with your focus. Make sure you keep those 'Me's' in check though. It's annoying when people always bring the convo back to themselves. Listening properly involves getting rid of any distractions – so no sneaky texting and no 'uh-huh' uninterested murmurs either, okay?

Your SASSY Charm School checklist
Don't risk being a Charm School dropout, here's what you need and how to get it...

Self-confidence – Love who you are. Stand up straight, be expressive, be passionate, know what you're talking about, move around to appear enthusiastic and lean slightly forward when talking to people – you'll instantly send 'I'm a fab person' vibrations surging through any room!

Make others feel important – Let people know they matter and that you enjoy being around them, develop a genuine smile, nod when they talk, briefly touch them on the upper arm, and maintain eye contact.

Genuine interest in others – Dare to care. Ask after a friend's brother if he's been poorly. Ask your colleague how her new puppy is doing. This will show how warm and friendly you are and that you actually remember and care about what's going on in other people's lives.

Generosity – You can be generous in lots of ways – if a friend is moving, offer your time to help her pack. If your bestie hasn't a thing to wear on her first date, offer her first pick of your wardrobe. Doing good things for others is a win-win situation, your friends think you're fab and you'll feel all warm and fuzzy for your good deed.

Most importantly, true charm comes from within, so find ways to be yourself and share your already rather wonderful personality with those around you!

Stage presence

Do *you* have stage presence?

While you may not want to rock out on a stage like a SASSY super-hero you should always be able to step into the pink-tinted spotlight and shine. The good news is that you don't have to turn on your most super-shiny, charming self all the time, especially if you're generally a shy girl – that would just be hard work – but knowing how, and when, to be your most fabulous self is a must-have charm skill. You don't have to be big-headed, show-y or arrogant to come across as confident and happy – no siree.

Every good SASSY girl should demand attention when she walks in a room, but she's never, ever rude and she most definitely has her glitter-girl egos in check.

Follow our SASSY sparkle steps to get the attention you deserve without screaming 'look at me'...

- Being a loud mouth *isn't* a necessity - *show* people what you're about, rather than shouting it in their faces.
- It may be tempting to try and bluff your way through a conversation. But if you don't know much about the subject being discussed, you'll get mucho more kudos if you listen up and ask questions.
  You can't lose – get your facts right and people will respect your wisdom, ask questions and people will appreciate your interest and honesty.
- Tone down your gossip factor – this will show that there's

more to you than people may think. Your mates will trust you with their secrets and your reputation will sky rocket. Gossiping gives out icky negative vibes. Don't do it.

- Choose things that you love doing and not because everyone else is doing them. If you're passionate about something, and enjoying it, you'll have more energy and people will be so much more attracted to you.
- Most importantly, be yourself. It's a fact, everyone is an individual and that's what makes you who you are, gorgeous girl. Be proud of why you're different, because if you love yourself up, other people will love and adore you too!

Body Talk

Our bodies can do a whole lot of talking without us saying a single word. How many times have you formed an opinion about someone without even so much as speaking to them? While it may seem all kinds of rude, it's a fact that a large part of the initial impression we create - some dudes in white coats estimate as much as 80% - comes from our body language. Make sure your body is talking all things SASSY by:

Facing Facts – your face is by far the most expressive part of your SASSY self so make a conscious effort to smile. Your grin is a killer tool, especially when you meet new people. It will help you to appear sparkly gorgeous, warm, open and friendly.

Nudge, nudge, wink, wink – Your eyes give lil' miss Sherlock-like clues to your emotions, so use them to express your interest in what's being said. When you make direct eye contact you will send a super-clear message to the person you're talking to that you're interested, calm and most of all, confident.

Giving good gesture – your hands can be much-o expressive too.

Wave them around like an out-of-control crazy windmill and you're telling the world you're a nervy girl. Instead, use wide hand gestures to imply that you're an open and honest person and small hand gestures when you need to emphasise what you're saying.

Tough talking – Do you ever feel like everyone wants something from you? And even though you want to say no, you actually say yes? Is it because you're afraid you'll hurt their feelings or upset people?

Of course, it's important to be a nice person, but sometimes people will take advantage of a sweet-girl nature and will walk all over you if you let them. The trick is not to let them. It's absolutely possible to kick butt when you need to, in the nicest possible way, of course, here's how to talk tough in *any* situation and remain super charming!

Borrow happy friends – They beg to borrow the cute-as-a-button new leopard print pumps that you haven't even worn yet, so you let them.

How to deal: If your friend still hasn't paid you back from the last time you lent her cash, and now she's asking again, or if your stuff keeps getting returned with stains – or not at all – and you feel completely taken advantage of, it's time to draw the line. If you don't, you'll end up resenting your friend.

Say *'I promised myself I wouldn't give any more loans until people pay me back.'* Or if it's an item of clothing or a DVD, say: *'I know you'd be careful, but I've decided not to lend it to anyone. I hope you understand.'*

If she's a real friend, she totally should.

Agony aunt – You're a good listener and love helping your friends out, but lately you feel like their personal agony aunt.

How to deal: If mates' problems are getting you down, it's time to let them know. It won't make you a bad person; it will just stop you getting mad at them.

Don't stay on the phone for hours when you don't feel like it, just say: *'I'm sorry but I have to go – can I call you tomorrow to see if you're OK?'* Learn to start saying how you feel. Being honest isn't the same as being nasty. Friendship is about give and take and you shouldn't have to do all the giving. Being strong will earn you respect.

Gossip girls – Get-togethers with your gal pals are starting to resemble the movie *Mean Girls*.

How to deal: When mates pressure you to be mean about a mutual friend who's not there, it can be hard not to join in – even though you know it's wrong. But remind yourself, if they bitch about her, they'll probably bitch about you too. That should make it easier to make a stand. The simplest way to protest is to say nothing. That way you'll have a clear conscience without losing face. But if you feel brave enough to say something, just say you'd rather not get involved.

Lil' miss let down – Your friend is so much fun to be with but you can't rely on her for *anything*. She's always late to meet you, forgets your birthday every year, and you're totally inseparable until a guy comes along, and then you don't see her for dust…

How to deal: A friend like this is rarely doing it to be mean. Usually, it's because you're letting her get away with it. So stop making excuses for her and don't accept a half-hearted apology.

Next time she upsets you, don't say: *'It's OK,'* say, *'Actually, I feel let down. It's not good enough and I wouldn't do it to you. Please don't do it again.'*

She won't change overnight and you might need to say it a couple of times before you get results, but if you make it clear your friendship needs to be earned, she should start to make more of an effort.

Word Weaving

When you want people to take you seriously, you've got to say it like you mean it. This way people will know that 'no' means 'no' and will be less likely to persuade you to say yes, because you *can* turn people down without letting them down and still remain your gorgeous SASSY self.

When turning someone down, use 'I' phrases like *'I feel...'* or *'I think...'* so they know it's a choice you're making for yourself and not against them and most importantly, don't feel like you ever have to apologise for saying no. Never say sorry for staying true to what you want.

One of the most powerful tools that I use when I talk is to simply start telling people what I want, instead of what I don't want. Basically, I've edited the word 'don't' out of my vocab.

Why is this so important?

Well, if I tell you *'don't worry about this, it's not difficult, it won't take long'*, what are you thinking? You're probably already thinking that it sounds like a big problem, right? It works the same way as if I were to say to you, *'Don't think about a pink car'* you'll immediately get a picture in your mind's eye of just that – a pink car, right?

It's much easier to make a mental representation of *'a pink car'* than it is of a *'not a pink car'* isn't it? In fact, it's almost impossible to make a mental picture of *'not a pink car'*. It's a mixed message. And not surprisingly, it generates mixed results.

So, stop using *'don't'* and *'not'* and replace them with *'do'* and *'is.'*

By doing this, you enable the listener to make sense of what you say in one easy step. They have a clear mental representation of what you want.

Here are some examples:

'Don't worry, it's not difficult' becomes, *'I know you'll find this easy.'*

'Don't forget the meeting tomorrow' becomes, *'remember the*

meeting tomorrow' or even better, *'see you at the meeting tomorrow.'*

'Don't tell the customer that we've messed up the order' becomes *'tell the customer that their order is delayed.'*

Now this particular kind of word weaving obviously takes a bit of practice. Many of us have grown up hearing *'don't'* and it's become a habitual pattern in expressing ourselves. To get out of the habit, practice using positive language when you have time to think about what you want to say, such as when you write an email or prepare a presentation. The more you practice when you have time to think about it, the more it will become an unconscious pattern in your everyday convo.

Channel your inner rock star!

If you were to look up super-cool music girls in the dictionary, you'd find pictures of Debbie Harry, Pink, Chrissie Hynde, Cyndi Lauper and Gwen Stefani, well, you would if you looked in my dictionary, anyway! Maybe you might have other pop, rock or super star types, but whichever shero-girls you dig, they all have one thing in common... the 'IT' factor. The 'IT' factor is one of those undefined and subjective attributes that you either have or don't. And for those who don't have 'IT' this undeniable 'IT' factor is more than just an attractive quality. The plain truth is that those who have 'it' are just like you. The difference is that they are aware of, and have practiced, and mastered, the fundamental skills of engagement. In a nutshell, this is something you can learn. Discover your own 'IT' factor by channeling your inner rock star!

Be YOU-nique – There are so many sheep-like people out there who all do, say, dress and eat the same things, that being totally original is pretty rare. Figure out what makes you different. Enthusiasm, being beautiful and graceful or awkward and weird, don't hide the thing that others might think is odd or different, emphasise it – that really is a sure sign of superstar behaviour!

Own the stage (or just the boardroom) – You can just tell by the way a person walks up to the microphone if they have star quality. It's the way they look out at the camera, or the crowd, before they've even played or sang a note – you can do the same. Make like a rock girl by walking tall, repeating *'I'm awesome'* internally, and making eye contact.

Don't be so serious – When you have a sense of humour about yourself and everything around you, you become insta-attractive girl. There's no need to be a full-on comedian to stand out, just be someone who is bubbly in spirit and humour.

Unleash your Sparkle

Oprah, Nelson Mandela, Obama and the Dalai Lama, these people have a powerful presence that helps them influence everyone whose lives they touch – how do they do that exactly?

Charisma.

Charisma is your ability to attract and influence others by way of amazing communication skills, empathy, charm and personality. True charisma radiates from an inner confidence about yourself and curiosity about others.

The word charisma comes from the word 'charis', one of the Three Graces in Greeky mythology, used to mean the divine gifts, or attributes we each have within. Charisma is in all of us, we are born with it, for sure we have to develop it, but mostly, we must rediscover and re-remember it. Deep inside, we buzz with love-stuff, energy, magnetism and vitality. When we connect with our SASSY self, when we banish the Funkatron and its thoughts of doom and gloom, we can tap into our enormous potential, and when we start to rock and rule at being us, we begin to let our inner charisma shine. It's as simple as this, when you believe you're kick-ass, when you follow your heart, when you share the love stuff, when you're good and true to yourself, you can connect to your natural charisma.

I love this particular SASSY super-hero-girl power because it's like the gift that keeps giving. You shine like the brightest star-shaped girl in the cosmoverse, and as you do, that focused energy of gorgeousness touches all those you chose to share it with, and then, because it's been shared, it comes right back at you. I LOVE that.

To put this into action, you need to get out of your head, and be in the moment. This is extremely important because being in the moment allows you to respond to what's happening in both a controlled yet spontaneous way. Whenever you catch yourself being in your head when interacting with someone, stop yourself and practice being present. Listen, make eye contact and really connect – simply feel the love, don't try to analyse it.

Boost Your Charisma

Whether it's a meeting, a pub or a party, be sure to enter with energy and purpose, as if you're a cowgirl in a Western movie walking through a set of saloon doors. Cowgirl costume is, as always, optional. Who doesn't love a cowboy hat? Or is that just me? It is? Oh.

Work it – Walk with confidence. Even though you might not feel it, if you stand tall, release your shoulders and straighten your spine – your body will communicate otherwise, you'll look and feel better, plus you'll breathe more freely and won't constrict your body's energy. If your body is in any way tense, it won't function properly, and this tension might prevent you from breathing calmly and evenly.

Even if no one's talking to you, glance around the room with interest, make eye contact and check out the art on the wall. You won't look uncomfy, you'll just look a little aloof and exotic and you'll have everyone whispering *'who's that girl?'*

Relax – When you speak to people, remember to breathe. A lot of people stop breathing or hardly breathe under stress, and go into panic mode or distort their breath. Try to get your breath as deeply into your body as you can. Keep your body open and breathe regularly.

When you speak, don't mutter, but don't shout either, look at the person you want to reach with your voice and both listen, and talk, to them fully. The most charming people I know are fun to be around. Simply being in their presence makes you feel better. With their contagious energy, they invite others to join their party.

A charm for well... Charm!

You will need:
A lion's head charm (buy or make one)
A yellow candle
Rose or orange essential oil

Buy, or make, a charm that resembles a lion's head. (It can be as simple as you want it to be, as long as *you* know what it is). Pass it three times through the flame of a yellow candle, meditating on your self-esteem and the respect you truly deserve. Then infuse the charm with your energy by anointing it with the oil and repeating a positive bravado boosting mantra like, 'I am feisty and fabulous' while you do it. Now wear it on a chain, or keep it in your pocket, then when you see or touch it, you will feel your confidence soar. I have mine on my keyring and anoint it at every full moon for a li'l extra make-me-feel-better-ness!

Lucky charms

To boost your super-hero-girl powers o' charm and good fortune, you'll need a lucky charm – an object charged with magickal powers. Without a doubt, the horseshoe is one of the most recog-nised symbols of luck in the world. Often brides will have a small silver horseshoe in their bridal bouquet and many farmhouses have at least one horseshoe over the threshold to protect them and bring them good luck. Tradition dictates that the horseshoe symbolises keeping the devil out and good luck in. How you hang it depends on where you live.

In most European countries, horseshoes are placed downwards so that the luck continues to pour down into the house. In Britain and Ireland, people believe that the shoe must face upwards, like a cup, or the luck will spill out. I have a horseshoe tattooed on my right arm, facing upwards of course, so that I always have my lucky charm with me, but if you don't fancy anything quite as drastic, horseshoes are easy to track down – try visiting a local stable and asking if you can make a donation in return for a worn horseshoe, most horse owners will be happy to oblige.

Other lucky charms include:

Four leaf clovers – they are considered lucky because they're so rare. Druids believed that if you found a four-leaf clover, good fortune would come as long as you kept it.

Rabbit's foot – The belief that a rabbit's foot can bring you luck originates from Africa. Folklore states that only the left hind foot of the rabbit is lucky and that the good fortune is only activated when rubbed.

Black cat – No-one is entirely sure where this tradition originated from; it's believed to come from 15th century folklore when black was the colour associated with Mother Nature. If a black cat crosses your path, nod your head and say thank you three times, this will increase your luck threefold.

A lucky charm is actually anything you are drawn to, maybe it's a crystal you've been given, a bracelet, a coin or a pendant, whatever you chose as your lucky talisman, simply charge it with luck and believe in it's powers. Soak your charm in salt water in the light of a full moon – this will charge your talisman and take away any negativity held by it's previous owner. Dry and place in front of a white tea light. As you light the candle, say:

'With this light, I ask the gods and goddesses to charge my charm with love and luck. So mote it be.'

Fortuna and the wheel of fortune

To boost my super-hero-girl powers o' luck and good-fortune, I call on Goddess, Fortuna. Most consider Fortuna as 'Lady Luck', but she is so much more than that. Fortuna heads up luck, fate, destiny, future-telling, oracles, kismet and chance, all the things that any good gypsy witch like myself simply loves. Fortuna rocks because she promises riches and abundance for those who believe in magick and have joyful intentions, which FYI, is every SASSY super-hero-girl – hurrah! If you ask this Roman Goddess of Luck to turn the Wheel of Fortune in your favour, she'll turn bad luck to good, attract fortunate circumstances, events, and opportunities, help you to nurture your destiny through the ups and downs of your life cycle and literally transform your life. Who doesn't want a goddess-girl like that on your side? The girl is kick-ass!

As I mentioned in a previous chapter, I love the tarot, and I always use the cards to help with spells, to connect with my spiritual homegirls and for guidance. When connecting with Fortuna, I use The Wheel of Fortune tarot card. The Wheel of Fortune, or *Rota Fortunae*, is a concept in medieval and ancient philosophy referring to the capricious nature of Fate. The wheel itself belongs to goddess Fortuna, who spins it at random.

Now, I know that's it's possible to create my own luck, but any action I take can be much more effective if it has the right energy behind it. Enter Goddess-girl, Fortuna.

I place the Wheel of Fortune card on my altar, I light a green candle, green is the colour associated with luck and prosperity, although she does rather like anything silver, gold, sparkly and fabulous too, and I call on her to sprinkle me with her love, luck, abundance and support.

Strange meetings, lucky breaks and chance meetings are all part of the Wheel of Fortune's influence, so, if you use your natural abilities and skills to their fullest, the benefit of the Wheel can make *anything* happen. Beware though, when Fortuna spins the wheel, you may find yourself living in a brand new city or even a new country, with a completely different career or a yummy new lover, run with it, I dare you!

If you feel like you're stuck in a place where nothing is working right, it is twice as important to focus on getting ready. Just like the Wheel shows, luck of all kinds is cyclical, and an upturn will always follow a low point.

That said; don't dread the times where you're not riding the top of the Wheel. A low point doesn't necessarily mean bad luck – it might be more of a static situation. That's the time to improve what you have.

Ask yourself:

Can you recognize a good opportunity in the present or is it often in retrospect?

....

....

....

What is your biggest obstacle to accepting good luck when it occurs? Did you ever have an experience where you took a risk that didn't pay off? Looking at that situation, would you say now that it felt lucky or unlucky?

....

....

....

If you had to pick one new venture that you feel needs a boost of luck, what would it be? On your end, have you done all the footwork and research necessary to run with Lady Luck when she appears?

....

....

....

The Wheel of Fortune tarot card connects you to the sense of luck that is smoothly turning through every life, connecting to Fortuna will assure that you get guidance, abundance and support as you rock out at creating your very best life. Get prepared to take what is offered, and use it to your best advantage!

Be a good luck magnet

I am often told I'm lucky. Apparently, I'm lucky because I've got an amazing boyfriend who is in love with me and I'm in crazy heart with him, I'm lucky because I write for a living, I'm lucky because I've had books published, I'm lucky because I've hung out with celeb-types, yep, I'm lucky, lucky, lucky. But what's the difference between them and me? Why do I seem so much luckier? Well, if you knew me, you'd know that all my successes, which others may view as luck and good fortune, stem from making wiser choices and taking action. It's what SASSY girls do; they create their own luck and don't leave their life to chance. That's right, you have far more control over luck than you think. Your luck, whether it's good or bad, is actually manifested by the way that you think.

Belief: Believing that you will get the things you want in life and deserve the things you want in life will make you more likely to receiving them. Why is this? Well, when you think about something, you see a picture in your head, when you have a picture in your head your mind is locked onto receiving it. When you mind is locked onto receiving something it will start, unconsciously, to notice ways of getting what you want. It will start to notice opportunities that you might have missed had you not had that picture in your head and the belief it could happen – this is where the real SASSY sorcery happens.

Taking risks: People who are lucky take more risks. They don't have to be financial risks, or risks that put you in danger, but pushing yourself outside your comfy zone, will open up a whole treasure chest of fabulous opportunities that you may never have experienced before. Unlucky people tend to be creatures of routine. They tend to take the same route to and from work and talk to the same types of people at parties. In contrast, many lucky people try to introduce variety into their lives. For example, one person described how he thought of a colour before arriving at a party and then introduced himself to people wearing that colour. This kind of behaviour boosts the likelihood of chance opportunities by introducing variety.

Working hard: You need to do the work. Very rarely does success and good luck fall in your lap, take a look at your favourite singer, dancer, artist or sport star, it may look like they've become famous overnight and are crazy-rich with lives of lux and good fortune. However, what most people don't see is that these same people have spent years of hard work and sacrifice to get to where they are today. My fave story is that of Sylvester Stallone. He famously auditioned with every casting agency he could, sold his dog because he was so poor, yet still didn't get a break. He didn't give up, he wrote a script for Rambo, and the rest, as they say is history. Working hard is a pre-requisite to being lucky. Fact.

Generosity: Being generous to others is a must-have trait of 'lucky' people. It doesn't have to be financially, although, if you can afford to you absolutely should share your wealth, it will come back to you ten fold, but generously sharing your time and knowledge will cause a bounce back of luck and good fortune too.

Instinct: Opportunities exist. Often they are right under your nose or banging at your door, but you simply haven't trained yourself to recognise them or act on them. How many times have you felt in your gut to go for something but your brain held you back and told you all the reasons not to do it? Be aware of your bodily sensations when you are thinking about trying something new. The more you trust your instinct the more it will serve you better. This just about trusting your instincts though, it's about taking action rather than procrastinating. Just do it.

Positive outlook: Change your thoughts, change your life. Simple as that. I've never met any successful person who thought the world owed them. Nor have I known any 'lucky' people who complained about being a victim. If your luck isn't what you'd like it to be, it's probably time for you to try on a new attitude, a SASSYtude.

SASSY-tude

So, there was a time, not so long ago, when the sorceresses, witches, and wise women of old, truly rocked and ruled. These kick-ass ladies lived on the edge; they saw the world from a totally different perspective. They dared to use their magick, and when I say magick, I don't mean the wand-waving abracadabra kind, although that's pretty cool too, no, I mean *real* SASSY magick – cleverness, cunning, intelligence, intuition and ohh la la sex appeal - to smooch, flirt and grab hold of pleasure, success and adventure, no matter what. So why shouldn't you do the same? Every woman, every person, for that matter, should rock their SASSY, create their own glitter-sprinkled road map and head straight for the direction of their dreams. That includes you. Yes, gorgeous girl, I absolutely, positively mean YOU.

It begins with SASSY-tude. A few years ago, I wrote a series of books for teen girls called *Think Pink*. The leading lady, Lola Love, discovered a pair of pink-tinted shades that switched her view of the world from drab to fab. Now, to develop a SASSY-tude, you need to take props from Lola and do exactly the same. You can pick your own frames, mine are a 1950's pair of vintage cats eyes, but when you start to see the world through SASSY lenses you work on the basis that something good, or something so much better than good, is coming your way at ALL times, because you, li'l Miss Fab, are in control of your own awesomeness dial. Whatever comes your way, can, and will, be used to make your sweet self the most beautiful shade o' happy. When you work your SASSY-tude, in every circumstance, YOU are the one with the edge. You know that whatever your desires are, they will not just be fulfilled, but they'll be blown out of the water by something substantially bigger and better.

Coping with bad luck

Bad stuff happens. Fact. It's how you deal with that bad stuff that matters. If something bad happens to me, I initially throw a pity party, but now instead of wallowing indefinitely, I always look at what could have made that situation worse. Instead of thinking 'oh why does this happen to me, I am the unluckiest person in the world, what's going to happen next?' I think 'thank the goddess, that could have been a whole lot worse, now what lesson can I learn?' I'm not perfect-o and some days those challenges will floor me, will totally knock me for six, but the important thing is to not let it become your story. It only becomes part of your story if YOU let it.

Get lucky

Join the good luck club, there's no membership fee, and you can be a card-carrying member for life, all you have to do is make a list of all the good luck that comes your way. Do it for a month. Start today. Make a list of the date and what happened, keeping a good luck list will help you focus and will train you to be on the lookout for chance events at all times.

Be aware – Be aware of your surroundings and always look around for opportunities to make things happen. Your awareness will help you to discover opportunities that others have missed.

Ask for, and offer, help - Ask for help when you need it and also reciprocate when others need help. When you're helping others, you tend to build up relationships with people who are more likely to help you when you need it.

Say Yes More Often – my bestie and I watched the movie, *Yes Man*, starring Jim Carrey, on a particularly glum day for both of us. It wasn't the best movie we'd ever seen, but after watching it, we both vowed to say yes a lot more often, and we've both had quite the life adventure because of it! We don't need to say yes to everything in life but by saying yes more frequently, more fun, adventure and opportunities will definitely come our way.

DARING DAME: Francesca Lia Block

If you like your fairytales with a touch of fantasy realism, Francesca Lia Block is your go-to girl. She creates amazing female characters who have real quirks, who don't quite fit in and make me feel less alone in the world. I remember when I first discovered her book *Weetzie Bat*, I devoured it in one sitting and then read it again. Five times. Her books evoke crazy emotion in me. She's a word weaver of epic proportions, she speaks beautiful truths that others would not dare to even whisper, and most importantly, she believes in love. Something you will experience on every single page, of every single book. Sigh.

FLB – I heart you.

You are an author girl of awesomeness, yet you're so much more than that too, how would you define yourself in the world?

Mother, first and foremost. Friend. Mentor. Teacher.

How do your own spiritual beliefs influence your work - does it inspire you to create in a certain way? Does it define the work that you do?

I believe that we are all connected, that we must honor each other, ourselves, the planet. I believe in love, equality and kindness. I believe that the love between some souls is so deep that it can never end. I believe that art and creativity heal. These things appear in all my work.

The city of Los Angeles is a character in itself in your writing. How does the city feed your creativity?

I have been here my whole life so it is naturally a part of me. I love the different kinds of beauty that reside here—the natural world, the world of artifice (a glamor the city puts upon us) and the dangerous, often toxic beauty that challenges me.

To me, your books epitomise magick in all it's forms - what does magick mean to you?
Magick = love.

You have characters with names like "My Secret Agent Lover Man" and "Witch Baby;" How do you dream up these characters?
I pull names from my sub-conscious but also from graffiti, signs and baby name sites on the internet. I am always keeping my eyes and ears open for wonderful new names. I used the tarot primarily in my book THE HANGED MAN. I structured the book around a tarot reading. I also use the cards to inspire students in my writing classes.

If your life were a movie, what 5 tracks would be on the sound-track?
>   *Very young* by Cat Stevens
>   *Winter* by Tori Amos
>   *Lust for Life* by iggy pop
>   *Breathe Me* by Sia
>   *Thank U* Alannis Morissette

But it changes all the time...

What are your thoughts on the term feminist, and would you consider yourself to be one?
I am uncomfortable with any labels. I believe in equality and consider myself a humanist if I am going to use any 'isms' at all. I have great respect for and gratitude to the feminist movement

for the changes that have come about because of it.

Weetzie Bat is your most infamous character, what do you think it is about her that keeps her completely relevant over twenty years after her first appearance in print?
I'm not sure. I suppose that she is truly herself and that she sees the magic in things no matter how dark they get, which is something that many of the young women who still read about her are also capable of, or need to be reminded about.

Do ever have any self-doubt or issues that have got in the way of your flow? If so, how do you deal so you can do your gorgeous thing?
I ignore them and forge ahead. The process of actually creating is more important than being good at it.

What's your:
truth? Love
motto for life? Love each other
secret to success? Work hard and don't give up
favourite book? *Never let me go* by ishiguro
most treasured item? Photos of my family, my mother's wedding ring, my father's giant blue painting of mysterious flowers.

To find out more about FLB and her books of wonder (FYI: if you only ever read one FLB book, PLEASE make it Weetzie Bat) head over to: **www.francescaliablock.com**

Cultivate your SASSY-tude

Being sensational is about feeling good inside and out. When your power of all things sensational switch is flicked to the 'on' position, you feel full of energy, bursting with vitality, you're in touch you're your desires and you're full of optimism. You should be feeling filled-to-the-brim with goodness and ready to take full responsibility for your health and well-being. That's when you know you've got yourself a delicious SASSY-tude to life.

So, how do you cultivate your SASSY-tude? Well, you need to fall head-over-Westwood-heels in heart with yourself and develop rituals of bliss-kissed loveliness. To do this, you'll need to go get your diary and book a date with…YOU.

De-stress your body

Before you begin, it's important to unwind and shrug off any burdens or stresses you might be carrying – a stressy job, hectic social life, demanding family - you should release any negative energy from the get-go. Allow me to introduce to you…exercise.

In the past, exercise and I were not what you'd call BFFs. There was absolutely, positively no love lost between us both. I dabbled. I even owned a rather lush black and pink tracksuit combo, but for the most part, I wore it whilst eating biscuits and sitting on the sofa. The main reason I didn't like exercise, was because I didn't want to sweat, I especially didn't want to sweat in public, which, personally, I think was a really rather valid reason for not wanting to exercise. Except the lack of exercise lead me down a not-too-nice road to depression, over-eating and self-loathing, and the further you head down that road, the harder it is to turn back. So the more depressed I got, the more I stayed in, the more I stayed in, the more I ate, and the more I ate, the more I hated on myself, it becomes a total rinse and repeat scenario.

Which is why, when the doctor encouraged me to take up exercise instead of prescribing yet more anti-depressants, I felt a little cheated. Are you kidding me? Do I look like I am capable of exercise right now? I'm depressed, I need to curl up in a ball and shut the curtains, not pull them back and let the sunshine in. Except that's exactly what I did. I started to walk. Yep, that crazy one-foot-in-front-of-the-other movement that I'd been doing since…well, pretty much forever. I'd been living by the sea, my favourite place in the world, and yet I barely went to visit, so as suggested by the doctor, I made a playlist of uplifting tunes (just the act of choosing songs that made me happy, brought a smile to my face – do it now, it's a brilliant insta-pick-you-up!) put on my tracksuit for it's *actual* purpose, and I went for a walk. I did that once a day for 30 minutes, and I can categorically say, it did more for lifting my depression than any drug I've ever taken, or any bar of chocolate I've ever eaten.

Now, I'm not playing down depression, far from it, it was a very dark and scary time for me, and I know that for lots of people, medication may be the only way forward, but for me, re-discovering the outdoors, pushing myself to step outside my door each morning and connect with nature, helped me to start travelling a more light-filled route to the happy stuff. People however, were a whole different story, which is why I wore my hoodie and headphones so I didn't have to connect right away, but breathing in the fresh sea air, feeling the sea spray on my face and taking out my headphones to listen to the waves definitely put me on the right track to recovery. Since then, instead of trying to do exercise that I don't dig, because really? What's the point? Life is far too short to be doing things you don't dig, I went out of my way to find forms of exercise that I did love, like dancing, swimming and yoga because, believe it or not, keeping fit and healthy doesn't have to mean gruelling hour-long workouts or an entire evening spent at the gym. Hurrah to that!

Just 30 minutes a day doing something to get your heart thumpin' is enough to get these feel-good benefits pumpin':

- A boost in your mood
- Stressy-messy feelings banished
- The risk of icky health-related illnesses – like high blood pressure, heart disease, diabetes and obesity are reduced, phew!

- You become super flexible – go, go, go flexi girl!
- You sleep better
- You'll have much-o energy

Exercise is the easiest way to improve your health and body shape: it will help you live longer, boost your super-hero-girl powers of SASSY and make you feel generally happier and full of energy – it also means you can, if you want, eat an entire chocolate bar completely guilt-free. Now, if ever there's ever a reason to work the junk in my trunk, that's most definitely it!

Get it on!

I am no gym bunny. Don't get me wrong, I *am* a member and I *do* go every week, but usually to use the pool because I love to swim, not to get my sweat on, I've tried, and I'll never say never, but right now, being a gym girl is not how I roll, but the good news is that there's a whole lot of other body-lovin' boosters that can leave you feeling fit, fabulous and full of energy – here are some of my favourites...

- Wanna kick some ass? A black belt is *so* this season! If you fancy doing *Matrix*-like manoeuvres to keep fit, high-energy martial arts can help build speed, strength and stamina. Karate, judo or Tae Kwan Do are just some of the martial arts on offer. Hiiiiiiii-ya!

- Get your skates on! Forget blades, I'm a retro girl, so I work my pink and cream quad skates like a wannabe pop princess working at the Hard Rock Café until she finally gets discovered. Roller-skating works your thighs, raises your heart rate and gives you the perfect excuse to wear your favourite circa 1972 outfit. Or is that just me?

- Yoga – like, ohhhmmm. By combining a series of bending

and stretching postures with breathing techniques, yoga not only improves flexibility, strength and muscle tone, it also helps you to chill your boots and manage a stressy, messy head. If you want to become a really bendy Wendy, I recommend Hatha yoga, as it's perfect for beginners. It's designed to be gentle and is suitable for people of all ages and levels of fitness, including a juicy me!

- Swim to win – Swimming is easily one of the best forms of exercise around as it promotes strength, stamina and mobility, resulting in all-round feel-good fitness. It's my absolute favourite thing to do; I was obviously a merm-girl in a previous life!

I also really recommend belly dancing, hula-hooping, pilates and bustin' a move at a street dance class – there are so many fun and fabulous ways to keep fit, I defy you not to find one you don't fall in heart with, but before you throw yourself into any crazy get-fit regime you're never gonna stick to, start by letting your body know your new 'I love me' lifestyle starts right here, right now, by:

- Making an appointment with yourself – at the beginning of each week, write your sessions in your diary, just like you would a hair-cut, a friend's birthday or a soiree. Treat getting fit like any other date and be sure to stick to it!

- Ask your friends to be cheerleaders – enlist their help to kick your bee-hind with 'go-girl' phone calls, txts and email reminders to work out.

- Make it fun – because you'll never fall in love with exercise if you hate what you're doing. Try everything from yoga to aerobics until you find something you enjoy. Try something you've never done before, dare you!

- Reward yourself – so you've stuck at your chosen activity for a whole two weeks? Well done you! Treat yourself to an DVD-athon, some cute workout pumps, or a day of pampering. When you treat yourself you're much more likely to keep up your activity!

Li'l Miss Motivator!

If you find the whole idea of doing physical activity semi-traumatic and want to throw a drama-laden hissyfit at the mere mention of the word 'exercise' (I hear you on that, by the way, I was exactly the same) you're going to need to channel your very own Li'l Miss Motivator. Tight-fitting lycra is, of course, optional. These are my personal bee-hind kickers, and I assure you, I absolutely need them, because it's easy to try things out, but in order for exercise, in whatever form, to become a regular part of your weekly routine, you're going to need to keep motivated…

- Break it down. You don't have to do exercise all in one go. If you can't face a whole hour, you can get exactly the same benefits by exercising sporadically throughout the day. Try jumping off the bus a stop earlier or walking 15 minutes to school and 15 minutes home. Before you know it, you'll have clocked up 30 minutes of exercise without even knowing!

- If you're a regular slouchy-couchy, start with something easy such as Speedy Girl walks – a short SG walk will give your heart, lunges and leg muscles a good workout. Start by walking for 5-10 minutes a day and build this up adding 2-3 minutes each time.

- Celebrate the benefits - along with being full of juicy

energy, you will start feeling less stressy and generally much more happier – yay! So when you notice improvements, register them, write them down and celebrate 'em, g-friend!

- Now this baby is guaranteed to get results – buy yourself a work-out ensemble. Except, the deal is, they can only be worn for exercise, NOT chilling on the sofa. If you're not a lycra/sports wear kinda girl, then make like me, and take gym-wear props from Miss Dita Von Teese. DVT is never seen looking anything less than glam, and while the same can not always be said of myself, I do like to maintain a certain element of style when keeping fit, so I wear an all black ensemble - lycra yoga or capri pants with a nice fitting top - and I team it with leopard-print Converse, a Land Girl style bandana for a li'l rockabilly chic, waterproof mascara and a slick of hot pink lipgloss. Voila! Changing into them, even when you don't feel like working out, raises the chances of you actually going ahead and breaking into a sweat – seeing as how you're dressed for it and all!

Work it, girl!

Okay, so if you're like me and you're not mad about getting sweaty Betty in public, why not rock on in the comfort of your own living room? There really is no excuse not to get into this exercise lark, my favourite thing to do when it's gloomy outside, is to channel an era-icon, download tunage and bust some era-related moves. BTW: I'm more than cool with you stealing my moves.

What you will need:
Floor space
Three tunes from your favourite musical moment in time

The ability to channel your favourite 'era icon'

Instructions:
Forget super choreographed shape throwin', this is all about bustin' some killer era-inspired moves for fun, with a whole lot of emphasis on the word fun, okay?!

1. Pencil three 'work it, girl!' sessions in your diary for the next week
2. Feel free to accessorise your comfy ensemble with era-related items
3. Before you continue, channel an era icon of your choice to maximise the experience
4. Now, shake your booty to warm yourself up, pop on your fave tracks and press play, sweet thing!

These are my era-inspired 'work it, girl!' sessions – who knew exercise could be this fun?

The rock-girl workout

Sample tunes:
The Clash – *London Calling*
Green Day - *She's a rebel*
The Ramones – *Let's dance*

Channel:
The skinny-hipped, Joan Jett. Love. That. Woman.

Favourite era-inspired moves – The Air Guitar

1. Stand with feet apart, turn left foot out at an angle and bend knee slightly. Keep right leg straight. Bring your left arm straight out to your side with your hand in a fist.

2. The next two steps should be done in a fluid motion. Swing your right arm forward in a circular motion; it should meet your left arm and continue round to make a circle. As you do this with your arms, kick your right leg across your left at an angle so it's even with your left arm.

3. Bend and lift your right knee until your heel lines up with your left knee and jump up and down on your left leg. Keep swinging your arm in a circle like you're a rock star thrashing her guitar! Repeat on the right – right leg bent, right arm out to the side. Do this for one minute each side to the beat of the music.

Mosh pit protection

1. Stand with feet shoulder width apart and knees slightly bent.
   Bring arms out to your side and bend them into a solid L shape. (Like you're showing off your rock-chick-hard biceps).

2. Clench your abs as you move your arms towards each other, in front of your face. Your forearms should be parallel.

Don't drop your arms between steps one and steps two. Try ten reps of step two. Do six sets, resting arms at your sides for a few seconds between each set.

The Dancing Queen routine
Sample tunes:

Abba – *Dancing Queen*, natch.
KC & the Sunshine Band – *(shake, shake, shake) Shake your booty*
The Bee Gees – *Night Fever*

Channel:
Agnetha and Frida complete with white spandex jumpsuits and a whole lot of hair.

Favourite era-inspired moves

The Pivot turn
Keeping your left foot on the spot, use your right foot to move your body round in a circle towards the left.

Take three steps to twist round 'til you're facing forward again.

Repeat x 5.

The Tap
Step to the left with your left foot.

Follow with your right, tapping it down next to the left. Clap twice in time to the music. Repeat to the right.

The Grapevine
1. Step to the right and take your left foot behind, bending your right arm at the elbow. Bring your left arm to meet your right and clap.
2. Step to the right, follow with the left foot (feet together). The move goes: wide step, cross feet behind, wide step, feet together.

Repeat on the other side.

The SASSY 'work it, girl' tips
- Always warm up and cool down with gentle stretches – this way you won't pull any muscles.
- If you feel any pain during exercise, stop!
- Drink water before, during, and after a workout.
- If you're poorly-sick don't exercise – it'll only make you worse.

- It's important not to get super obsess-o with exercise; we all need a healthy balance.

Now, if you're still trying to resist, at least give going for a short daily walk a go. It's one small addition to your lifestyle that can impact on it more than anything else. On many levels exercise is a must, but it's ability to relieve stress, prevent illnesses and improve body function and tone are great reasons to get you out there. Walk briskly, and walk to the point of being out of breath, I begin each day with a walk as it charges up the brain and stimulates the body, seriously, just do it. You'll thank me, I promise.

Eat yourself gorgeous!
Now, while 10% of your awesomeness is down to exercise, a whopping 80% is down to what you put in your body. (FYI: the other 10% is down to genetics and g-friend, we can't do anything about that!) My body is not, and never will be, celebrity-girl shaped. It is however, Lisa-shaped and finally, after years of not loving the skin that I'm in, I adore it. So when I eat food, I make sure it's the *right* food.

It's simple really. I dig on me, so it would be completely rude and wrong to fill me up with super-addictive junk food – it's called junk for a reason, y'know! Now, I'm not saying I'm perfect, I LOVE food, Nigella is my homegirl, but when you're SASSY you have to develop a healthy 'tude to food. The payback? A healthier, even-more-gorgeous-if-at-all-possible YOU!

A healthy 'tude to food is completely necessary if you're to become the very best version of you that you can possibly be.

Start by saying 'No' to:
Crazy crash diets that just don't work – really, they don't and they won't.
Takeaway/fast food/chocolate bingeing – binging on processed food is not good for your body *or* your self-esteem.

Starving yourself – depriving yourself of food will just make you want it a whole lot more, so when your body eventually gives in, which it always will, chances are you'll overeat the stuff your body craves most, like fatty and sugary foods. Boo.

And instead, say 'Yes' to:
Listening to your body – your bod is super-clever and has subtle ways of telling you it disagrees with your food choices.

Eating breakfast – don't skip breakfast as it will make your stomach growl like a monster-type later in the day.

Healthy food alternatives – replacing the family pack of biscuits with five servings of fruit or vegetables a day.

Ditch the Diet
Talk of all things diet-related is to be ditched right now, because quite simply, diets suck.

Especially the A-list style crash diets that promise you a better body in two weeks. They really suck the most. In reality, all diets *actually* do is make you into a grouchy, queen of angst. When you deprive yourself of serious nutrients that your body needs to function, and endlessly calorie-count and scale-jump, it's more than enough to make a girl take a trip to glumsville.

I hate to admit it, but I've been a complete sucker for the crash diet in the past. My worst one was the 'No Carbs' diet, where you basically replace carbohydrates (bread, pasta, rice, potatoes) with high-protein, high-fat foods like meat cheese and eggs, the theory is, your body's fat-burning process turns to high-speed, making you an instant girl of slim and slenderness.

Wrong.

All I got was an achy belly and really beyond-bad breath. I am not exaggerating when I say people kept their distance from me for the entire week that I was doing it, I hummed! But that's what happens when you cut something really important out of your diet, your body sends out a message that it's not happy. For the record, carbs aren't the enemy. In fact, 'no-carb' diets aren't good for us girls full stop. Our bodies need carbs for energy. Y'see, diets are bad, so no more mention of them, okay?

You decide!

When you're SASSY, *you* make the decisions about what's right for yourself. *You* decide whether to devour an entire family sized bar of chocolate in one sitting or whether to instead, have a couple of 70% cocoa chocolate chunks as an extra-special bite-sized treat. *You're* in control, sweet thing. Yep, your friends and family will always look out for you, but ultimately, as I said before, you are responsible for number one – you.

I was the official chow-down girl when it came to eating an entire king-sized bar of chocolate in one sitting. I would go into a chocolate-induced trance, not even tasting it until the final bite. That was because I was living in I-don't-dig-me-ville. Every time I felt sad and glum about not having enough money, or something that had happened at work, or the size of my bee-hind, I would throw myself a full-blown pity-party and would make myself feel better by chomping on chocolate. I would instantly feel guilty and turn into my very own number one hater, dissing on myself so bad that I'd have to go eat another bar of chocolate.

This was not cool. It created a circle of misery that I couldn't seem to escape from. It kept my vibration low, and meant that all the big visions for my destiny that I was creating in my head, weren't developing, they' weren't being nurtured because I wasn't giving myself enough self-love to make that possible. Instead, self-pity stepped in, and I'd find myself saying, 'Why bother?' or 'it doesn't matter, I'll always be fat and unhappy.' It's not until you realise that you are fabulousness in a YOU-shaped package and that YOU are the one in control that you can start to switch it up. Yep, I could decide to eat a king-sized chocolate bar, but I could also decide *not* to as well. It was a revelation!

I tell you what else has totally rocked my world o' eating, and that's cutting out the likes o' white bread, flour, sugar, rice, milk, cakes, pastries and biscuits. I know it sounds like I'm totally depriving myself of all the 'best' food, and there's a time I'd absolutely have agreed with you as these used to be my total go-to foods for happiness, yet none of them are actually real. They're all man-made with processed products. Now, I'm no food expert, (although since becoming a girl o' SASSY I've actually started studying nutrition – SASSY girls are clued-up girls. Fact.) Our bodies just don't know what to do with processed foods, so it stores them as fat, not cool. The ideal situ would be to ask yourself, before you eat any food, does this food rot? Could you eat it raw? If you answer 'yes', then hurrah and happy dances, your body will know *exactly* what to do with it. If however, you take a look at the ingredients and there are words that you don't recognise or you can't pronounce, chances are it's processed, which means your gorgeous body simply won't know what to do with it, and will store it as fat. Research has linked the consumption of processed food to obesity and their intake should definitely be reduced, or ideally eliminated. That isn't to say you can never have them again, but once you start to cut down on these, foods, you'll notice a difference, I promise you. In fact, if you try these super-food fixes, you will have be glowing inside and out...

Fruit = glow-girl skin
For skin that sparkles, eat lots of berries – strawberries, blueberries and blackberries. They contain anti-oxidants that protect skin cells from damage and help make you a gorgeous glow girl!

Oily fish = luxe locks
Eating salmon, sardines, tuna or mackerel will keep your hair as

shiny as one of those badly dubbed girls on the shampoo adverts. These fish contain lots of protein and omega-3 fatty acids, which moisturise your tresses from within. Happy hair swishing!

Oats and nuts = energy

Swap sugary-sweet cereal for porridge – it's the perfect start to the day. Porridge really is a food o' fabulousness because it releases energy slowly and will keep away those mid-morning chocolate cravings.

Bananas = happy belly

Poorly digested food can sit in your belly and make you feel allsorts of icky but the potassium in a banana will mop up excessive fluids reducing any uncomfy feelings. No more impromptu exits from fab soirees due to icky bellies – yay!

Eat a fortifying breakfast

As well as a glass o' orange juice to boost your vitamins, start the day with a bowl of porridge or oat-based cereal sprinkled with nuts and seeds. Oats are high in fibre and release energy slowly, so you'll feel full for longer. Add a mix of sunflower, pumpkin and hemp seeds, which are all a great source of omega 3 fatty acids – essential for regulating hormones and maintain the body's organs and systems.

Listen to your gut

Really take time to get to know what your body actually needs. There are two go-to books that have completely changed the way I eat and think about food and they're *Slim for Life* by Jason Vale and *Crazy Sexy Diet* by Kris Carr. Both are filled with information about the way that the food on our supermarket shelf is *actually* created and how most of the things we've been taught about nutrition are based on research by big companies who obviously want us to buy their food. It's so important to get educated about what you're putting in your body, you ever heard that saying 'your body is a temple'? Well, when you're SASSY, you worship at the 'temple of You' everyday. What we do to our body, or put into it, is a reflection of how much we dig ourselves. So, it makes a lot of sense that if you want to look and feel, fierce and fabulous, you have to treat your body with respect and keep it in perfect-o working order. Right?

I have never been a domestic goddess, yet, when I started to take an interest in what I put into my body, learning to cook seemed like the next natural step. Now, while I'm not rushing to throw a dinner party and cater for a gazillion friends and family members, I am really rather proud that I can create healthy and yum-filled food from scratch now. If the thought of creating in the kitchen fills you with dread, start with my personal favourites – Bars o' Yummo – there's no cooking involved, they're packed full o' goodness and taste dee-lish…

Bars o ' Yummo

These Bars o' yummo are great sweet treats and full of good-for-you niceness – win!

INGREDIENTS

Peanut butter – 1.5 cups
honey – 0.5 cups
sunflower/pumpkin seeds – 1 cup
oats – 2 cups
sultanas – 1 cup

WHAT TO DO:

- mix together all the dry ingredients
- microwave the peanut butter with the honey in bowl for 1 minute
- mix the pb & honey combo well
- Pour over dry ingredients and mix well

- pour into dish and press
- wait 'til cool, cut up and munch – yummo!

Keep yourself hydrated

Okay, if there were just one single, solitary thing you could do to show your body the love stuff, it would be to drink water. I know it sounds silly, but I have spent a LOT o' money on beauty prodz, and the only time my skin has been as clear and English-rose-glow-y as it is now, is since I stopped drinking any kind of cordial and fizzy pop and made sure I glugged 8 glasses a water a day. Fact. I know it sounds boring-snoring, and I'm not going to lie, to start with, so did I, but the results speak for themselves. I know it sounds all very angelic-like, and believe me, I'm really not, but I'm all for an easy life and if simply drinking 8 glasses of water flushes out my system, makes me feel fab and my skin look awesome, then it's a no brainer, surely? You'll notice that by simply reducing your intake of caffeine and alcohol, which both really dehydrate you, and replacing them with plenty of water and herbal teas – limeflower and chamomile tea are my faves – that your body will blow you thank-you kisses right from the inside.

Enough, already

The saddest thing I experience in my work is the incredible skill that lady-kind has to talk trash about their bodies.

So much time and energy is wasted thinking they are 'not enough', convincing themselves that they're repulsive, that they don't measure up to other people's expectations, so much so, that it affects how they dress, how they hold themselves, how they interact with others and how they let others treat them.

Enough, already.

I mean it. We need to call a truce with our bodies and create a huge-ass fest o' love. I'm not saying I look in the mirror and love my reflection every single day, but I do give it a bloody good go.

Every day I work at accepting my body for how freakin' awesome it is, what it does for me and most importantly, how I allow myself to talk about it. I've absolutely positively banished the word 'fat' and 'ugly', I appreciate my body just the way it is. Not in half a stone's time... Right now.

Do the same. I know it's scary, but it's all down to you. It always is. Change up your thinking, show yourself some love, think of all the kick-ass women who have gone before us and if in doubt ask yourself what would................(insert name of your chosen goddess-girl, woman o' awesomeness here) do? If your list o' awesome girls are anything like mine, I'm pretty sure they wouldn't be dissing on themselves, they'd put both arms around themselves and show themselves, whatever shape or size, love. Go on, do the same. You absolutely, positively owe it to your SASSY self.

Pampered Princess
The act of bathing and showering should be the most decadent time of a SASSY girls day. It's your opportunity to cleanse, stroke and caress your gorgeousness, thank your body for its awesomeness, whisper sweet nothings in its ear as you lavish yourself in delicious products and prepare yourself for the day ahead. Yet so many of us simply jump in the shower because it's what we 'do' each day.

A morning shower is my absolutely non-negotiable practice of self-love every day. I love to connect with the water, feel it cleansing away any ickyness from the previous day, I use gorgeous smelling prods, some of which I make myself, and I lavish them on my skin, I feel my curves, I love my curves, I take the time in the shower to give thanks for my body, just as it is. I might sometimes get mad at it for not looking, or being the way I'd like it to be, but right in that moment, I show it nothing but love. Even if I'd like it to be fitter or more toned, unless I love it, just as it is, I'll always be in conflict with it.

Fall in love with your body, show your body love and you will *only* want to do delicious things to, and for it. It makes exercising, pampering and choosing the right foods to put inside you far easier than if you were doing it from a place of grr-ness and self-loathing, and I am ALL about making this thing called life easier.

As you're drying yourself and rubbing lotions or sweet smelling potions on your body, whisper it sweet nothings. Tell your legs how thankful you are that they hold you up all day, thank your feet for allowing you to wear, and walk in, those beautiful heels, whisper extra sweet nothings to the curve of your hip for adding a special amount o' sass to every step you walk. Author Julia Cameron says 'there is a direct connection between self-nurturing and self-respect' and she's so right. When we nurture ourselves and show ourselves love every single day, we start to respect the gorgeous girl staring back at us in the mirror. She's truly sensational. YOU are truly sensational.

Brush it, baby

I recently became curious about the act o' drybrushing not only as a spiritual act o' self-love, but as a way of releasing icky water retention and getting your blood pumping in the right direction. I love a multi-tasking activity. So, I got my neekid on. Ohmystars, it's now my number one pampering treat. Grab a fluffy towel, a long handled dry brush from the chemist or superstore, and some bathroom time.

On dry skin, work up from the soles o' your feet using long, gentle sweeping strokes, then move onto your hand, arms, tummy and back, finishing with the neck and scalp. As you do it, I whisper sweet nothings to each body part, 'thank you legs for holding me up and for being long and lovely', once brushed, oil yourself before taking a shower. I love nothing more than a sweet-smelling oil, but recently to save money, I bought a huge bottle o' wheatgerm oil which is AMAZING for nourishing skin. It doesn't smell too yum though, so I add a few drops of my favourite essential oils, bergamot and grapefruit – insta-firming oil for not too many pennies.

Make your own facemask
You can make a hydrating facemask with the ingredients in your fridge, budget-friendly and good for you too. Simply mash up half a banana and mix with a tablespoon of honey and a tablespoon of milk. While it may be a delicious treat to eat, I highly recommend rubbing it on your face, leaving on the skin for 15 minutes then rinsing it off. Yes, you are totally allowed to lick your fingers!

Take a soothing soak
An Epsom salt bath, is a great way to detoxify, relax muscle tension, and soothe aches, pains and inflammation in your body – can't you hear your body breathing a sigh of delight at the idea of something so lovely? Epsom salts have a sedative effect on the nervous system, so they will also help you get a really good night sleep too. Alternatively, you could pop two drops of relaxing lavender and camomile essential oils into a cup of milk and pour into the bath as you run the water. Next light a candle, or if you have an essential oil burner, add two drops of each of the oil to the burner then lie back and enjoy, letting your mind, body and soul be soothed and relaxed. Ahhhhhh…

Apply a slick o' lipstick
As I've mentioned throughout the book, I have a few connection processes that I really love, like: listening to my favourite go-for-it girl songs that I LOVE to play at super-high volume because they always change my state from 'meh' to 'I'm freakin' awesome', journalling three pages of automatic writing each morning to clear my head space, going for a walk in the forest, swimming and doing my *pilates for indie rockers* DVD, but I was really struggling to find something I could do absolutely every

single day, no matter what, that would raise my energy, change my state into '*I mean business, damn it!*' and mostly make me feel sensational, because really, that's what it's all about. When I feel good, I do good.

As I work from home, I sometimes have a tendency to pull on a very comfy pair o' very unflattering leggings, a hoodie and scrape my hair back in pony-tail. Dita Von Teese I am not. Seriously? Have you seen that girl at the gym? Amazing.

Anyway, while you'd NEVER catch Dita in comfies, it got me to thinking about my absolute love and passion for make-up and how the act of applying lipstick alone, is like an actual sacred practice for me. Does it raise my energy? Absolutely. Does what colour I choose to wear affect my mood and how I act? Hell to the yeah. So today, before I sat down to write, I have applied a delicious slick of Rockalily's *Rockette Red*, blown myself a little kiss in the mirror and told myself I'm foxy. Superfluous? Yep. Has it upped my awesomeness for the day and made my sensational levels sky-rocket? You betcha baby!

DARING DAME: Star Khechara
Allow me to introduce Star. She's a hula-hooping, book writing, skincare making, workshop teaching, jewellery designing, burlesque performing, age defying, rawfood making, beauty guru. Not only is Star a total poster-girl for being sensational – look at her, she's freakin' divine – she knows what foods can be put on our skin, and in our bodies, to make us all look and feel sensational too. Not only that, Star is totally kick-ass at all things turn-your-life-around-able. Once you've read this you'll have NO excuse not to be your most sensational self. Star, I heart you!

Describe yourself in a tweet (140 characters or less)...
Fruit-loving, hoop-dancing, skincare-making, booking-writing, workshop-teaching, steampunking eco-fairy.

What is it you do exactly, Miss Star?

I do so many things, as someone recently said, I have a 'portfolio career', which sounds a lot better than 'this 'n that'. I love life and trying out new things and studying so I have built a life around several of my favourite hobbies-cum-businesses. I run a nutritional website called The Facelift Diet which teaches people how to eat themselves younger, sexier and vibrantly healthy. As The Facelift Food Coach I write books and articles on this same subject and also teach yummy 'facelift food' workshops. I am also a skincare expert and I teach the science of organic skincare formulation at School of Holistic Cosmetology. I have a passion for plants – whether for medicine, scent or to eat. I am also an artist with a degree in applied arts, I make quirky jewellery from odd things, found objects and recycled metal – as you can see I am an eco-diva. I am a natural show-off and enjoy performing on stage doing burlesque or hoola hoop go-go dancing.

How did you discover your passion for health and well-being?

I think it discovered me! I can't remember a time that I wasn't ecstatic about nature, at first it was animals and I regularly brought home stray and injured animals - even a horse once. As I got older I concentrated my energies on the plant world and became fascinated by herbs. At age 18 I trained in Aromatherapy and was so excited about working with the essential oils, I quickly discovered that I didn't enjoy giving body massage but loved studying the science of the oils. I started to create simple aromatherapy blends and then skincare products and natural incenses. All of my spare money went of oils, extracts, essences, butters and waxes as I toiled over my bubbling cauldron. About the same time I became interested in food and nutrition; already a vegetarian, I discovered a book 'Raw Energy' one day and just thought 'wow'. I threw myself into being a 'raw foodist' and bought my first juicer. My thirst for knowledge grew and I eventually went to university and college to study nutritional medicine. To this day these subjects fascinate me.

I love how you've made all the things your passionate about, actual jobs – how did you discover that this was possible and most importantly, how have you made it happen?
Well at first I didn't think I could, I come from a very poor background and my poverty consciousness followed me into adulthood. I spent years in jobs I hated because I thought I 'couldn't' do my passion and make enough money from it. I started reading lots of positive self-help books which gave me insight, but still nothing really shifted for me, somewhere I know I was blocking the idea of success. I continued in a string of awful jobs until one day I woke up and just 'knew' I deserved better. Finally I felt like I deserved success and to make a living following my passion. I just decided from then on I would not do anything at all unless I 100% loved it. This wasn't actually that long ago and I have come a long way in a few short years! I have had no financial backing from anyone and I found, since I made my decision, that enough money often appears just at the last minute as long as I keep focussed and not fall back into 'it's not gonna work' attitude. Believe me, if I can do it ANYONE can. Basically I just made my passion my priority, I live and breathe it every single day and I try not to worry too much about where the money will come from.

What's been the biggest challenge for you creating your work-girl niche?
The biggest challenge was me. I kept getting in the way of my own success by pre-empting that it wouldn't work and then getting in the way of the success path by giving up. These days my biggest challenge is to stop myself working too hard! Because my business is also my personal passion it can take over, I have had to learn to say 'no' to people and projects that I am not 100% into as they detract me from my passion and end up taking over.

I used to do a lot of free work all the time and it left me too exhausted to do the work that brought me an income, so no matter how 'nice' I want to appear I have to be firm and say 'no' if I want to keep my sanity.

You're also a hula-hooping burlesque queen – Where do you think the current trend for all things burlesque and vintage has come from and what do you love most about performing?
I honestly have no clue where the burlesque resurgence has come from, I guess it's tied up in the trend for retro and vintage lifestyles. I think maybe modern life feels too clinical and minimalistic, so people crave the frivolous glamour that these past eras have. I am a natural show-off, I feel so excited to be on stage and to be entertaining people through dance/performance. I am not such a fan of all the backstage stuff like endless chore-ography but it's all worth it to step out onto the stage - as soon as I step out, the face goes on and no matter what I was feeling before the performance, it all melts away in that moment on stage. It's always over too quickly.

Can women really have it all?
No one should try to 'have it all' it's good to not have everything you want as it only creates the desire for more. I think these days women are encouraged, no expected to be all things to all people; the perfect cook, perfect mother, perfect host, perfect body, perfect lover and always look good, smile, earn money... ad nauseum. I honestly don't think that we can be all of these things and be happy too; and what a straitjacket to place on ourselves! Women should just be free to pick and choose - hey I am a rubbish cook and I hate hoovering but I make an awesome face cream and you should check out my hoola hooping ;-)

What and who makes you jump in the air happy?
My boyfriend Louis, my fruit delivery, sunshine, getting a

publishing contract, stepping off stage after a performance and life in general – I am quite excitable.

What's the best advice you've ever been given?
A poetic friend once said, after I was pacing about saying, what shall I do? *'Do nothing. Human being you are, not human doing.'*

What's your life motto?
It's really very simple "Have fun" oh and "I'm too old to grow up now"

If you had a super-power what would it be?
Ooooh, it would have to be breathing underwater, not very 'super' I know but I could indulge my childhood dream of being a mermaid

What five tracks would be on a Star soundtrack to life?
  Royksopp - *What else is there*
  Red Hot Chili Peppers - *Can't stop*
  System of a down - *sad statue*
  Nancy Sinatra - *Summer Wine*
  Lamb - *Heaven*

What's your favourite:
Book: The China Study
Food: Mango
Movie: Stardust
Lipstick: Une (natural make up company)
Song: Lily, Rosemary and the jack of hearts (as sung by Joan Baez)
Quote: 'Practise random kindness and senseless acts of beauty'
Place to hang: South Spain
Website: Youtube - for random time-wasting

What does the term 'sassy' mean to you?
Super sexy diva with all round sparkle!

Isn't she acecakes? Total inspir-o-girl! To find out more about Star, visit her at: **www.thefaceliftdiet.com**

YOU

"...Stop searching here and there,
the jewels are inside you..."
Rumi

So, remember I mentioned a Paris trip, a trip that introduced me to my true SASSY powers? Here goes.

Paris est une fete.

My bestie and I were in total heart with Paris. We ate in the *tres* swanky restaurant *Kong* because we'd seen it on episodes of *Sex and the City*, we ate Nutella-filled crepes as we walked the streets of the Latin quarter, but the night before New Year's Eve, after a rather lovely evening spent watching dancing girls in nothing but frilly knickers at the *Crazy Horse*, we both decided that we wanted our lives to always be this magickal, so over a glass of cheap French wine, we wrote a love letter to the universe. Under the light of the gorgeous, sparkly Eiffel tower, we shared our hearts' desires, our biggest dreams and asked to be sprinkled liberally with a substantial pinch o' Parisian magick, because really, if any city can pull off a magick trick as big as hearts' desires and beautiful make-it happen dreams, it was Paris.

I've seen *Amelie*, I've seen Moulin Rouge, they're two of my favourite movies, magick happens in Paris. Fact.

Paris, I am glad to report, did not disappoint.

The very next day, New Year's Eve, the sun was shining and the air was full of sweet-smelling croissants as I took the metro into central Paris. Except today was different, today it was as if, at the strike of midnight, I'd become a magnet of complete and utter fabulosity. By beautiful happenstance, I met the gorgeous jewellery designer, Marine Chotard, creatrix of *Miss Sugar Cane*, (which is now a gorgeous boutique shop that can be found at 43 Rue Des Dames 75017 Paris, if you're ever in the city you MUST go visit Marine, her creations are *bijoux fantaisistes!*) I received compliments on my attire, from complete strangers, was offered a free taxi ride, and got a bag of free gifts from Sephora for being 'pretty in pink', and later, in a rather fabulous you-only-read-about-stuff-like-this-in-chicklit found myself hand-in-hand with an Italian male model taking a guided tour of the city, we shared a kiss under the Eiffel tower and he whispered sweet Italian wordage to me whilst walking down side streets in the city o' love. Sigh. I had to ring Miss Aimee to make sure I wasn't dreaming. Miss Aimee and I then went onto see the New Year in together with a bottle of cheap plonk in Montmartre, and were accosted by delicious French men asking us to dance. We'd literally become Parisian starlets. Ohh la la!

At the time I think we were both completely freaked out by the power of the Parisian magick, but now I can see that it was clearly combined with a whole lot o' SASSY-fication, which, quite frankly, is a magick all of it's very own.

We had aligned our SASSY – we'd connected with the universe, we dug deep down into our souls and declared, under that sparkly Parisian night sky, our truth, our hearts desires – excitement, adventure, delicious moments that will make our hearts thud, we believed that we were totally worthy of such lip-smackingly delicious good stuff, that our go-for-it girl juice was full-to-the brim, there was just no way in the world we WOULDN'T attract awesomeness in all its forms. If I'd been keeping a lucky list over those four days, I could of filled an entire notebook, finding euros, people going out of their way to help us, we even got told how *très magnifique* we were at Jim Morrison's graveside, how entirely appropriate that is, I don't know, but a compliment should always be accepted with grace and a smile. When he broke into a rendition of *'Come on baby light my fire'* we did however beat a hasty retreat.

What I didn't know on that magickal trip is that I was on a one-woman search for SASSY. I was desperate. I'd dabbled in spirituality, I was far too fearful to speak my truth, I thought sensual meant slipping into a satin baby-doll and talking in hushed tones, and sensational? Well, I played at it, I knew I had womanly charms, but I was most definitely not using them to start a revolution, that's for sure. It wasn't until I stopped looking externally for pleasure and joy, and sat still, really still, and listened to the beat of my beautiful big heart that I realised every-thing, and I mean EVERYTHING I ever need is already inside me and that I am capable of becoming the mistress of my own delightful destiny simply by creating it with my mind.

Now that's *real* freakin' magick.

Life doesn't start when you're thinner, have more money in the bank, meet your soul mate or buy a house. It's all about RIGHT NOW.

With a regularly cultivated SASSY-tude, you can radically change your life. So get good at it. Practice it. Find out what makes you feel the most SASSY and do more of it. Tell your gal-pals about the awesomeness that is SASSY, share the goodness, because the better we get at it, the more heart-led revolutions we can start.

> *"...There is not one big cosmic meaning for all, there is only the meaning we give to our life, an individual meaning, an individual plot, like and individual novel, a book for each person..."*
> **Anais Nin**

Create your own bespoke SASSY plan

I'm not here to give you a success manual for life, there are shelves and shelves of those out there already, being SASSY is learning about your own brand of SASSY sorcery, your very own gorgeous girl magick, your own super powers and creating your own bespoke SASSY blueprint (or in my case, pinkprint) for life.

So pull on your favourite ensemble, what you wear on your date with destiny is entirely up to you, it could be a fluffy white bathrobe, *What Katie Did* underwear, or your favourite PJs, or nothing but a diamond encrusted tiara, the important thing is that you try out, dip your toe into, and indulge in as many of the activities that I've intro-ed you to throughout the book s'far, they will activate your SASSY in a million different ways, align your physical, emotional and mental goodness, and help you unlock yet another SASSY super power; self-love. Sigh.

SASSY tip: The important part of making a date with your destiny is to make sure you spend the entire date indulging in YOU, so that by the end of your retreat, you are able to know what makes you happy, what makes you feel distinctly fabulous and create your own rituals o' SASSY self-care that will then become part of the only list I will EVER actually encourage you to write and stick to, and that's your ABSOLUTELY NO EXCUSES MUST DO EVERY DAY SASSY LIST (Catchy title, eh?)

You are what you think you are
Your thoughts are energy and are magnetic. You attract directly into your life what you're currently thinking and feeling. So if you're constantly putting out negg-o vibes by hating on someone, or thinking that life has dealt you a bad hand, you'll attract much of the same. But if you give out love stuff, expect amazing opportunities and actively seek the good stuff, you attract that right back to you. Sound simple? That's because it is.

It's the Law o' Attraction, it's ancient magick, but believe me, that stuff freakin' works.

Where is the love?
I mentioned earlier that love is the answer, no matter what the question, because it's the truth, it's MY big truth. I give love in big and crazy complete abundance, to my beau, to my family, to my friends, to people who's work I dig, I show mad passionate love to people who are making a difference in the world whether it's saying thank you to the dude that collects my bins, chatting

with the lady in my local convenience store, thanking courageous women for being beautiful beacons o' light or sending Gary Barlow a tweet to thank him for being my teen crush and still being so humana-humana hot right now. I don't need a reply or a response, although if GB did tweet me, I'd do a happy dance like no happy dance you've EVER seen before, I simply do it because I want to share the love stuff. Call me a hippy if you like, but getting into the kindness habit is a far better option than surviving on a diet of cynicism and toxic thinking. If someone does something that you like, tell them. If a shop assistant is extra smiley and polite, or a meal is really yumm-o at a restaurant, share the love stuff, baby and tell 'em!

Sadly, we live in a world where sharing the love stuff so openly may lead people to think you either have a hidden agenda or you're doing narcotic drugs, it's just not the norm to be selfless. Except when do you think SASSY girls do what's considered normal? Er, like... NEVER. Send out love stuff like you life depends on it. Mostly, because it does. Don't be false, or use it in the hope of getting something in return, that'll just lead to bad ju-ju later and no one wants that. Just send out love like a gazillion heart shaped red balloons on Valentine's day, 'cept don't wait til V-day to do it, do it every day.

What are you waiting for? Send an email to that blogger you completely love, give your partner a kiss, buy flowers for a neighbour and leave them on their doorstep with a note that simply says 'you're loved' – connecting through love each and every day is one of the most beautiful powers a SASSY super-hero-girl could ever own.

"...Everything that happens to you is self-created. Whenever you're responding to any situation, whether it's a sip of coffee, or a traffic jam, or a love note, or criticism from a boss, or rainy weather, you're in fact responding to a signal that you generated within yourself..."
Deepak Chopra

Manifesting Maven

I've pretty much been a manifesting maven for as long as I can remember, except I didn't know that's what it was actually called. My first experience of this magick jiggery-pokery, was when I was 7 and on holiday at Butlins. I was about to take part in a donkey race and I wanted to win more than anything in the world, I remember crossing my fingers so hard and repeating in my head, *I've won, I've won, I've won,* I kept repeating it until I crossed the finishing line and got my hand on that 1st place rosette. I kept doing it for the rest of the holiday, and it turned out that pretty much anything I focused on and believed in hard enough *actually* happened. I was like Sabrina the freakin' teenage witch.

What I didn't know back then was that there was more to it than simply crossing your fingers and saying what you wanted. Fast forward to 2010.

I was on a dating sabbatical. I was 31 and despite discovering my SASSY, I was feeling jaded by love. I'd been on a succession of dates that went from the sublime to quite frankly, the crazy-ridiculous. So instead of getting hooked on the endless dramarama that comes with dating, is he going to call? Are we exclusive? When is it okay to fart? You want to put that *where*? I jumped off the dating treadmill of doom and took a step into the world of me.

It was scary at first,

I was flying solo.

Any decision I made was purely my own. It was incredibly liberating for those 6 months not to worry about anyone else apart from me. I wrote a book proposal, I spent time with my friends, I read books, I travelled, I walked on freakin' fire, I immersed naked in the White Springs at Glastonbury, most importantly, I re-discovered Lisa. It was after the immersion, that I had my epiphany – I was ready to date. But this time I would be dating with the purpose to find my dream dude, the man I was going to spend the rest of my life with. I knew that this might mean having to kiss a few frogs before I found my prince, but that was okay, because I felt like Wonder Woman on a mission to create my own romantic destiny. Minus the hot pants and shiny cape, obviously.

My own ultimate super-hero-girl power? Make it Happen Moon Manifestation.

I'd created a form of manifestation that was working in other areas of my life - I got a contract for the book proposal I'd pitched, I was writing for magazines that I love, I was starting to get fit and healthy – so I decided to modify it to help me to find this man of wonder. I waited until the new moon on July 11th 2010, lit some candles, whispered some magic words to the Universe and set out my intentions for the moon phase ahead. I wanted to find love. The kind of love you only read about. I DO believe in fairy-tales and wanted to create a love story of my own that would rival anything Disney could muster. I got REALLY specific. Hair colour wasn't important to me, but the fact he would support me in my creative dreams was. What clothes he wore didn't concern me, I wanted a man, not a boy, who had the ability to love and be loved in return. So, I wrote this all down in yet another rather beautifully decorated love letter to the universe, I also made a little mojo bag filled with a crystal, my wish to find love, various love-inducing herbs and anointed it with a scent that I created specifically to attract love. I placed the list under my pillow and carried the mojo bag with me every single day.

I then got to work. Every morning during meditation, I would visualise my dream man and the things that we would do together. I asked friends to set me up on dates, and despite my initial trepidation about online dating, I even joined a few dating websites. I made a few connections online, none of which rocked my world, I also went on a blind date set up by a friend which was a complete disaster, then, exactly one moon phase later, at the next new moon, I had a message in my inbox from this rather delicious 6ft 6inch hunk of yummyness. He was masculinity personified and I loved how he described himself as 'honourable' and 'courageous' so I replied. Instead of rushing to meet, we spent two whole weeks exchanging emails, it felt romantic and decadent and my heart did a double-thump each time I found a new message from him in my inbox. Other people messaged, but I wasn't interested. I knew he was The One. When we eventually did meet, it was like a scene from an old romance novel – our first kiss was at dusk on a beach, he told me he loved me on the 3rd date, and six months on, we moved in together. At the risk of being vom-inducing, every day IS a fairytale. He has every quality I outlined on my list during my New Moon Manifestation and I thank the universe every day that we exist on the same celestial plain because he is the most amazing man I could ever have wished to meet.

Following my own New Moon Man Manifestation success, I was quick to share my method with other girlfriends, and my gorgeous friend Diane after suffering a hard break up, decided to give it a go too…

"…I'd been crying endless tears for the heartbreak and confusion I was feeling about a recent break up, I cried tears on Lisa's shoulders and together we discussed how powerful manifesting can be. Lisa told me about her own successful New Moon manifestation and convinced me to stand in my own power and create my own destiny. I left Glastonbury that night with an absolute sheer determination to really take a hold of my life. Though I had always performed my own New Moon meditations, this time I planned to do things just a little differently!

For two weeks every day before, during and after the New Moon, I took time out in my day to imagine how I wanted my life to be and not just write a list. Over those two weeks, I not only imagined my new life but I truly, truly believed it too. So much so, that I could picture what I wanted to draw into my life. I imagined my house sold and being free of the financial burden and baggage that this house represents and I imagined the man I wanted to meet. By the time the New Moon occurred, I could close my eyes and see very vividly the man in my life and his warmth and love and smile... I even smiled back at him as I created his image.

The night of the actual New Moon I carefully prepared all day and my intent was far beyond any strength I had felt before. I took time to focus completely, warning my family and friends not to phone and created my sacred space without apology.

This is where my story changes... Everything I set out to manifest on that new moon came true. Within a few weeks my house sold and best of all, I met the man of my dreams. He IS the man I saw as I focused on my intent over those weeks and on the day of the New Moon. I couldn't have been more specific about the man I wanted in my life right down to the way he looked, the way he smiled at me and his character and his goals in life. And the man I have met is all that I asked for and more! So loving, adorable, wonderful, genuine and intelligent – oh and well lush!

I would say to anyone who starts to wonder if they will ever meet the man/woman of their dreams, that yes you will. You have to really want it, be prepared to accept it and to never falter away from your dream! Now, as part of every New Moon Ritual I give my heartfelt thanks to the Universe for the gift of love that we have been blessed with and I will be focusing on our future..."

Isn't that simply dee-lish? And the good news is that it doesn't just apply to the hot love stuff, you can create everything that shows up in your life, you are the mistress of your life outcomes, so make them big and juicy, g-friend!

How to manifest
Before you create your list, ask yourself the following:

1. Believability: do I really think that my dreams are possible?

Because if you don't, the chances are they won't be

2. Limiting Beliefs: what are some of the beliefs I ma, ... adopted in my past that no longer serve me? Recognise the things that are holding you back, then let them go.

3. Commitment: how committed am I to attain/attract my desires? You've got to step up and show the universe you mean business.

Examine your actions and behaviours – are you sending out mixed messages to the universe? If you would like to meet someone, go out, tell friends that you want to, go online, attend gatherings, put yourself in a space in which the universe can send someone to you. Sitting alone at home and complaining about being single does not show the universe you are serious about putting yourself in alignment with meeting someone. Turning away dates and online dating match ups without even a single try also shows a lack of commitment in your willingness to experience what the universe has to offer.

Write down what you want. The best way to do this is to write in the present tense, and to start with the sentence, *I am so happy and grateful...* After that you can fill in the blank. *I am so happy and grateful that I am spending my life with a man who loves and understands me. I am so happy and grateful that I am in a loving, respectful and fun relationship.* BE SPECIFIC. Use words that have energy and meaning to you!

Mind movie

This is one of my favourite manifesting technique ever. Create a movie in your head of the things you want, and play it all the time. Every thought you think is like playing a tiny movie in your mind that floods your subconscious. The more you see something in your mind, the more real it will become to you. Create a movie in your head, get fully immersed in the experience – don't just watch it passively, FEEL how you would feel if this movie o' manifestation were real! Going on dates to the movies, hand in hand walks by the sea… This should be exhilarating, you should love doing it and relish every moment.

TAKE ACTION

This one is in all capitals because it is the most important part of all. Pablo Picasso is known for having famously said, *'Inspiration exists, but it has to find you working'*, now this, is actual manifesting fact. The universe needs to know you're serious, and that you're willing to put the work in. So, don't just sit back and wait for life to happen TO you, become the creatrix, baby!

Manifesting is doing the cosmic two-step with the universe. It's about doing the work, seeking opportunities, following your heart and having faith that things will work out for the best. It's about knowing that what you want is most definitely coming to you, but that you have to be the one to lead on the universal dance floor. If you just spend time thinking about what you want, but don't get out there and take any kind of real action, you'll be forever on the sidelines, it's time to get in the game! Remember: what we think, eat, drink, say, watch, listen to, read, focus on ALL affect our powers of manifestation, so be sure that what you're putting in, is going to up your vibrations and make sure you're super-magnetic to the good stuff.

Affirmations

In order to change your beliefs and create a new SASSY reality, you have to bombard your subconscious mind with thoughts of your desire. The best way to power up your intentions is to set up specific statements that will add a substantial helping o' awesome to the creation of your SASSY pinkprint. Your brain doesn't know the difference between real and made up, so as long as you give a clear statement of intent, it'll believe you. I love it!

Use the present tense If you say, *I will be rich*, being rich will always be in the future! The subconscious mind tries to literally bring about what it is asked to do. So if I say 'I am rich' or 'I choose to be rich' So make it active, like you're doing it already.

Make it personal. Include your name in the statement, it makes it real to you.

Be specific. Seriously, the universe isn't judg-y. You simply get what you intend, so be specific.

Be clear about what you do want, rather than what you don't. Concentrating on lack will bring about lack, we want abundance baby! So instead of saying I don't want a boyfriend who doesn't love me, your affirmation would be, 'I have a loving relationship with a boy who I love and who loves me in return.'

KISS. Keep it simple, SASSY! Don't complicate it, be specific and keep it short and sweet so that you can repeat it, read it, sing it out loud every single day.

The more you tell yourself that you already have the thing you desire, the more you'll believe that it's true and the easier it will be for the universe to help you bring it into reality. Think about, bring about.

Boost your SASSY powers
Many people go through life not really appreciating the skills and talents they've been given. Think for a minute about your daily routine; what do you enjoy doing and think you're good at? If you're not sure, ask others; often they'll see things that you might not recognise in yourself. Include personal traits, such as being kind, a great listener or being charming, but also think about the things you *actually* do. Perhaps you rock at making cupcakes, or can wear a pair of heels for an entire night out, or maybe you're super-sporty? Make a list.

Think about how you can take this a step further. What can you do to put these skills to use? If you're good with people and enjoy listening, perhaps you might want to volunteer for a charity or helpline? If you're imaginative and writing is your strength, you could take that a step further and join a writers' jam. Soon your SASSY pinkprint will include all the ways that you can develop your inherent talents and become super skilled. You are an untapped resource of total possibility – how exciting is that?

What's your passion? I'm talking real heart-squeezing passion that makes you feel like you want to do what you're doing forever.

....

....

....

What are your unique talents?

....

....

....

What achievements are you most proud of in your life so far?

....

....

....

Now get to work, li'l Miss Sherlock, and take a close look, are there any patterns? What gets you goosebumpy with excitement just thinking about it? Keep that excitement, hold it in a tight bear hug and use it as the fuel you need to fully rock your awesome.

Be your own super-hero-girl
I don't want to rain on anyone's fairy-tale parade, but no-one is coming to save you. This life of yours? It's all down to you.

So you know what to do, you know that how your life rolls has a LOT to do with the choices you make, you know that letting the emotions and thoughts of others affect how you see yourself is a problem and that you have to get that stuff untwisted. So what's left?

The work.

I've mentioned it before and I'll mention it again. The work is where the good stuff happens. You won't feel awesome 100% of the time and if I'm really honest, I don't think we ever actually stop doing the work, but if you're you in need of more cash, then start working on that. Do you need to get fit? Today's the day.

Super-hero-girls like Wonder Woman and Super Girl suggest that people are weak, and need super-hero-girls to come save them. This is totally NOT true of SASSY girls. We are our own super-girl-heroes, we're sheroes.

It's all inside you. You know what to do.

It's quite a lot of pressure being a super-hero-girl though, right?

Wrong.

All super-hero-girls mess up. In fact ALL superheroes mess up. Check out Batman, it was clear the dude had some kind of issues that he hadn't dealt with in therapy. However, super hero types do their very best. They realize that they are the only ones who are going to answer the call. YOU are the only one who will answer the call. You've got to step up and step out. They pick themselves up after every failure – as should you, rethink things as fast as you can, then seek the next best approach if Plan A fails.

You don't have to wait for someone to save you. You're the super-hero-girl.

Give yourself a name, mine is:

SASSY – The Go For It Girl – defender of positivity with the power to achieve amazing things!

Method of transformation: pole sliding and spinning in telephone boxes are not altogether practical and, lets face it, have all been done before so I simply click my hot magenta painted manicured fingers.

SASSY – The Go For It Girl - Superhero powers:
    Turning a negative situ into a positive
    Giving things a go
    Not fearing failure
    Being confident
    Taking chances
    Creating opportunities
    Making my own luck

Optional extras:
    PMA – Positive Mental attitude in a bottle
    Go-for-it girl juice – a freshly made shake with chutzpah and

courage, all a girl needs to do ANYTHING!

Glitter gun – the perfect way to bring fun and sparkle into your day

Lipgloss – why wouldn't you?

A positivity magnet – to attract nothing but the good stuff

Go-for-it Girl's mantra: Live life NOW!

Don't be afraid of the mirror

Take time out every day to look at your gorgeous self. Acknowledge your features. Smile at your reflection and say *'Why darling, you look simply ravishing today!'* or *'I love being me, I'm fabulous!'* Give yourself a cheeky wink and say *'I'm beautiful!'* Extra marks if you do it three times and say it out loud! Usually we look in the mirror and notice all the ways we aren't beautiful. This supports a culture that says who we are is not enough. And it's time to show ourselves that we are. If you're SASSY and you know it, blow yourself a kiss – mwooooah!

Another thing you can do for extra SASSY prowess is tap into your mer-girl power. I am obsess-o about mermaids. I heart the water, and fancy myself as a bit of a burlesque-y mer-girl. The mermaid is an important feminine archetype – alluring and sensuous, independent and courageous, self-assured and heroic. She's definitely as complex as a human woman, often helpful, but sometimes harmful. If you honour femininity as intelligent and spiritual, as well as sexual and beautiful, you too will dig on mermaids as inspir-o role models.

So, how can a girl incorporate mermaid-y allure into her look and life? Well, everyone knows that mermaids are the divas o' the deep. Their supernatural allure means they're irresistible to human folk, so use mermaid magick to give your own beauty a boost.

Mirrors are associated with mermaids, who were known for their gorgeous hair and were often painted brushing it. This simple beauty ritual will help you get in touch with your inner mermaid.

You will need:

4 drops of essential lavender oilSmall bowl of fresh water
1 hand held mirror
1 comb

- Add the drops of lavender to the water and stir. Take the mirror in one hand and gaze into it. Smile and watch as it lights up your face. Notice how fabulous and you-nique you are.
- Now dip the comb into the water and begin to comb your hair. Say, 'Mermaid diva deep inside, do not shelter, do not hide. Release your power, help me shine, from this moment on in time.'
- Keep combing until every strand is covered in scented water. Admire your reflection and recognise your inner beauty. It's a good idea to keep the mirror separate from your every day beauty essentials. Wrap it in black silk, and whenever you need to feel good, take it out and do the ritual, or just take some time gazing into it's depths – hey, good lookin'!

Find your signature colour
Think about the hues you like and those that make you feel super confident. I have a penchant for all things pink, but rarely wear it as a block colour, instead I clash hot magenta accessories with every ensemble. I even wear hot pink underwear under an all-black combo to give me a boost of *I know something you don't know* confidence. Choose a colour to match your mood, or better still, choose a colour that matches the mood you'd *like* to be in. So if you have an important meeting, a slick of red lipstick might give you an extra boost of chutzpah, or if you have a long work day ahead of you, wrap yourself up in an orange scarf – the possibilities are endless.

Red – confidence, passion and drive
Black – power, protection
White – cleansing, uplifting
Orange – enthusiasm, energy
Yellow – charm, joy
Turquoise – creativity, communication
Purple – psychic ability, adventure

DARING DAME: Kitty Pinkstars
If ever there was a girl who lives life by her own set of rainbow-painted rules, it's the deliciously delightful creative-girl, Kitty Pinkstars. I ADORE Kitty. Her daydreams and huge imagination help her to create things of cuteness that make people smile – I defy you NOT to want to join her as she rides her unicorn to adventure. Jump on board!

Describe yourself in a tweet...
I came from another planet. One day I will go home. I'm a contradiction. I'm sunshine AND thunder clouds. I make rainbows. I dream BIG!

What is it you do exactly, Miss Kitty Pinkstars?
I'm an artist in my own funny little way... I make and draw things, to get them out of my head, that helps make room for other things to come in through my imagination. They are inspired by my childhood, where I've been, and where I want to go, creating my own little world!

What I love most about you is your sunshiney disposition and attitude to life - where did it come from and how do you maintain it?
I had a magical childhood... I have always felt the power of a positive attitude helps you through all sorts of things tremendously! I am grateful for all I have and I see magic in the little

things in life.. I feel connected with nature and when I feel the stress of life getting me down I head to the beach to watch the waves or for a walk in the woods... Taking photographs is an amazing therapy!

I love how you've made all the things your passionate about, actual jobs - how did you discover that this was possible and most importantly, how have you made it happen?
If you asked me as a child what I wanted to do as a job I would have said I wanted to draw and make things. I sometimes sit now and think WOW I am living my dream. It's not always easy and I have to be strict as I'm such a daydreamer, but I started it as a part time hobby and it just gone from there. A lot of ideas, hard work and positive thinking!

Can you share any daily practices that you do to ensure you stay so deliciously positive?
I take a photo from my window every morning, I draw a doodle diary, I take time to think about what I have and how lucky I am, I surround myself with things I love, I NEVER take myself too seriously! And my house and wardrobe is PINK! That works wonders!

What's been the biggest challenge for you?
Believing in myself. It looks like it all comes easy! But that would be a lie, I have doubts and worries, I'm a terrible worrier but I use my creativity to help me deal with it!

G-friend, your style rocks – who are your style icons?
Eeek... Well I have recently had a complete style makeover, inspired by vintage old movies and classic movie stars! I don't have any one person in particular... But I want to bring back style and femininity in a tomboy way!

How do you handle critics?
It's THEIR opinion and I never take what isn't mine!

Can women really have it all?
Can anyone? If anyone can, then of course I believe woman can have it all, but it's always lovely to not have to do it all alone, huh?

What and who makes you jump in the air happy?
My family, my pets, my friends, rainbows, clouds, the seaside and a plan coming together...

What's the best advice you've ever been given?
Just be YOU!

What's your life motto?
Be honest, be true. Live it, love it. Just be the best version of YOU that you can be!

If you had a super-power what would it be?
I would be like Doctor Doolittle and able to talk to the animals!

What five tracks would be on a Kitty Pinkstars soundtrack to life?
Anything and everything by Counting Crows, my favourites are: *Black and Blue, Have you seen me lately? Perfect Blue Buildings, Baby I'm a big star now, Chelsea...*

What's your favourite:
Book: The Solitaire mystery
Food: Pancakes
Movie: Me and You and everyone we know
Song: Have you seen me lately? Counting Crows
Quote: "I don't want to have to do this living. I just walk around.

I want to be swept off my feet, you know? I want my children to have magical powers. I am prepared for amazing things to happen. I can handle it. "

Place to hang: My sofa

Website: Flickr

What does the term 'sassy' mean to you?

Living life to the full... Not being held back by fear or inhibitions... Being yourself and loving it!

Go check out Kitty's world o' wonder, it is the most gorgeous shade o' pink, and she makes the prettiest things, paints the prettiest pictures, and is so sweet she gives me toothache! **www.kittypinkstars.etsy.com**

THE ABSOLUTELY NO EXCUSES MUST DO EVERY DAY LIST o' SASSY

Now, without further ado, it's time to make, write and sprinkle with glitter your ABSOLUTELY NO EXCUSES MUST DO EVERY DAY LIST o' SASSY. Put everything you're going to do, each and every day to show yourself the love stuff. Make the creating of your ABSOLUTELY NO EXCUSES MUST DO EVERY DAY LIST o' SASSY a gorgeous creative process, pour a glass of wine, put on your favourite music, write it in gorgeous pens, illustrate it, cut pictures out of magazines, make it a piece of art and either pin it to your wall, or like me frame it in a completely over the top pink ostentatious frame, so you can see it every day and gaze at it's wonder.

Now do it.

Do everything you've put on your list.

Every day.

Start with one day. Don't feel overwhelmed, Just do it for a day, and then another, then pretty soon, once you get into a comfy rhythm with your list o' SASSY, you'll be surprised how easily it becomes part of your daily routine. Take it step by step, and don't be hard on yourself if you lose your way.

I like to make sure that I do all of the things on my list at least once a day, because I know that when I do, my energy vibration is higher, my light shines brighter and I have a SASSY glow that you'll only ever see on a girl who is fully in love with herself. My ABSOLUTELY NO EXCUSES MUST DO EVERY DAY LIST o' SASSY reads a little something like this:

- Make a juice or smoothie for breakfast each morning
- Orgasm
- Write in my journal
- Sing
- Pull a tarot card for guidance
- Dance – either to the beat of my own drum, a song on the radio, or while I'm baking cupcakes – just shaking the junk in my trunk makes life better
- Shower in sweet smelling products of deliciousness and thank my body for being awesome as I cleanse it ready for the day ahead
- Apply lipstick – Rockalilly lipstick in *Rockette Red* is my power-girl colour, I can totally take on the world in that baby
- Smile – it's the perfect-o accessory because it goes with absolutely everything!
- Light a candle and chat with the Goddess
- Do some yummy yoga stretches

If I do lose my way – which I sometimes do, I may have super-hero-girl powers o' SASSY but I'm still human, y'know – I can always get straight back to showing myself the love stuff with a quick read through and butt kick - hurrah!

Go for Gold
Take a look at anyone who has achieved success in some area of

their life, and you will see that the main reason for that success was an unshakeable belief in their idea or ability to succeed. It really is that simple.

Be your own cheerleader – enlisting a troupe of over-enthusiastic pom pom girls to support and motivate you on a daily basis just isn't practical, so make sure you say positive butt-kicking things to yourself everyday. I sing 'Lisa, you're awesome, you write words o' wonder and you've got amazing bangs' to myself every morning without fail. The tune often changes, and sometimes I add a new line, maybe abut my new nail polish or a job I've done really well at. Try it!

Take risks – it pays to take chances, because the only wrong decision you could make would be not to make one at all.

Face your fears – whether that's a person, or a task you've been dreading, or whether it's much bigger, feel it and deal with it. That way you can heal it too, and when you heal it, that's when the magick happens, baby!

Don't sweat it if you fail – it's not a failure, it's experience, learn the lesson and move on!

Crack the whip, you're the mistress of your destiny – do the work, tap into your magickal powers and make it happen!

DARING DAME: Dame Darcy

Dame Darcy is a renaissance girl o' magick and wonder. She's an illustrator and fine artist, a musician, doll maker and designer. Penguin released a new edition of Jane Eyre heavily illustrated by her. She has an etsy store where she sells prints and original art, dolls and other handcrafted work. She's contributed to the Tori Amos comics anthology, Comic Book Tattoo. Her other books include: Gasoline and Frightful Fairytales and they are beautifully terrifying and so delicious I want to lick them.

Her work is inventive, gothic, pretty and grim, she's a total risk-taking Rita who self-published before being recognised for her crazy-mad skillz. She is SASSY, she's a porcelain doll and I am in LOVE with her book: *Hand Book for Hot Witches*, which she described as a "Girl Scout guide for the apocalypse/field guide for the deflower." Come meet her, she'll mesmerise you with art-girl gorgeousness.

You started self-publishing at 17 – what was your first publication, why did you create it, and what gave you the chutzpah to make that happen?

By the time I was 17 I had already had a lot of really crappy day jobs. I knew that if I didn't get started on my art career now, no one would do it for me. I also knew I was going to draw and write comix whether I was going to get paid or not, so I might as well get paid to do the thing I love. My Mom told me, when I was about to graduate school, that she believed that I would be a successful artist, she just didn't know how I was going to be marketed. She also said that, as an adult, a lot of people spend most of their time working so I should work doing the thing I love. I believe this is sound advice and that when people follow their passion, they will never be led astray.

I started writing little books, fairytales and ghost stories when I was a really young kid. I think the first book I wrote was when I was 2. Seeing the sequential pictures, Great Grandma taught me how to read and write when I was 3 and I attribute the fact that I write as my career (despite my dyslexia) to her setting my brain like a broken leg correctly at this young age before it was to solidify into full blown 'not able to read' dyslexia.

I was raised on a beautiful horse ranch in the mountains of Bone Idaho partly, but lived in an ugly prefab looking town a lot too. My Dad is an artist, and I worked with him at his sign-painting shop as an apprentice until I was 16. This helped me understand how an artist gets freelance commissions and how to handle a career in the arts as a reality, he also gave me the skill sets of drawing, painting, story crafting, sculpture, poetry and music.

When were you first published?
When I was in High School, my comix were published in the school newspaper (Idaho Falls High) winning first place awards 3 years in a row in Northwest newspaper competitions with other schools.

My comic strip was called *Tumor Humor* and it was about the town I lived in after the Nuclear Power plant blew up. The scenario was that when your boyfriend picks you up for a date, he can see where you live because you are glowing in the dark and when you run your fingers through his hair it falls out, and when you kiss? You end up with each other's teeth in your mouths.

Not a popular topic in a Republican/Mormon town where over half the families work at the Power Plant. A lot of people hated my comics, but despite the controversy, this was clearly my direction, seeing as I was a straight D student otherwise.

How did you make it work for you?
My Mom knew I wouldn't be able to get into a normal college so she helped me get a portfolio together the year I was to graduate, and shopped it around to fine art schools so I could get a scholarship.

I ended up going to the San Francisco Art Institute, which was my first choice and I was so happy. It was a miracle, because up until then I was living in a very conservative small town in the middle of the Rocky Mountains, not near any big cities or culture. I went to a mullet gun-rack truck school where I was threatened every day by jock/hicks and had the minimum wage after-school jobs. I was such a horrible teen though, I feel bad for all the times I ran away.

When I went to SFA, it was like a dream come true. I had just been handed thousands of dollars to live in Bohemian Francisco, hang out with the children of millionaires, to do art and music and party. The second month away from Idaho, living on my own, the biggest earthquake happened since 1906, which cracked my school and turned the parking lot asphalt into an ocean wave. It also destroyed the Bay Bridge and burnt down Presidio and Berkeley.

In a way, my culture shock absorbed the earthquake, so I was OK. I started playing banjo in the band Caroliner Rainbow, which is still together in SF now, with its seven thousand five hundredth members. My boyfriend at the time and all the band members were older than me, and they showed me how to self-produce records and comics and through them, and my school, I knew people to hook me up with free photocopies, distribution and mailing.

I self-published two issues of *Meat Cake* this way, and began work as a freelance artist. By the time I was 21, I got a publishing deal with Fantagraphics to publish *Meat Cake* so I moved to New York City to continue working as a freelance artist. When doing lectures or classes, I always say, *'where there is a will, there is a way'*. If you want to do it, this is the sign that it is your destiny, and there is no such thing as failure. Academia and the arts are a way out of poverty or any compromising situation, you just have to make your own key.

You still self-publish now despite being published by big-shiny publisher-types too, why is that?
The spectrum of publishing is like a rainbow with self-publishing as one of the stripes, and getting published by big companies like Holt and Penguin on another, with all the other colours in between.

I like to do all kinds, from being commissioned to illustrate other people's books, to hand painting and collating my own books, to getting advances for bigger deals because it gives me autonomy. But it's also fun to work with other people in different capacities as well.

Usually the people who commission me are like minded souls who would be my friends anyway, and I feel so lucky and blessed that these magic people find me and come to me from all over the world to work with me. I have all my books on my site **damedarcy.com** and in my Etsy store **damedarcy.etsy.com** as well as hand made items.

I am a complete comic-lovin' girl. You create kick-ass illo's for graphic novels/comics, yet this is traditionally seen as boy territory - how did you get into it, and how do you find working in a supposedly boy-dominated industry?
I like creating female lead characters and having them have fun together from a girl's point of view.

So much of the entertainment industry sees women in a secondary and submissive role, when more of the populous of this planet are female, our point of view should be consistently and accurately represented.

In a way, being a girl cartoonist is cool, like being the last unicorn. But in another way, because I am not part of the boys club, I know that a lot of the pitches I've made didn't go through because, as I was brazenly told once to my face by a big entertainment company, *'If we market something to boys everyone will buy it, but if we target market girls, the guys wont buy it.'* Which is completely wrong, because a lot of my readers are guys too and by the way, there is such a lack of content, especially for girls, so why not CORNER the market? I know I want some one, and somewhere, to turn to and look up to, to confirm who I am and my place in the world and self worth.

I know so many other girls feel this way too, that's why I do

what I can to create this place in book, movies, animation, mu
and other multimedia, so It can manifest in reality.

Just because this is a challenge, doesn't mean I will ever give
up. I'm going to kill them all through kindness and I know I am
doing the work of the Goddess so the law of the universe
protects and guides me. I was born a girl in this time and place
to help utilize my skills towards aiding Mother Nature and all
women through this new revolution towards eco-feminism and
global consciousness.

**Not only are you an illo-girl, you're a fashion designer, a
musician, a film maker and a gazillion other titles o' awesome
- how and why do you follow quite so many paths o' creativity?
Do they all fuel each other? Are some more important to you
than others?**
My Dad said to pick the one I was best at for my career and the
others secondary as hobbies, or to help promote the main one.
That's why I mainly do drawing, but the others, like crafting,
painting and music are outlets and also help bring in other
income. Rock shows and cabaret are fun ways to promote books,
and film/ animation can combine all the creative elements of
storyboarding sequential art, doll crafting, music, costumes,
working with other people etc.

**How do your own spiritual beliefs influence your work - does
it inspire you to create in a certain way? Does it define the
work that you do?**
It is so much easier to have fear than faith. Faith takes discipline
and is an effort of your will. The word 'fear' stands for *False
Evidence Appearing Real.*

Which means 'fear' is just in your mind. Don't look back, just
look to what you have now and what you can do now, and do
what you are supposed to do every moment, of every day, and
you can't go wrong.

n voices in my head at every given moment and
song playing in a loop on repeat, plus noticing
everyone and everything all around me.

meditations and techniques to quieten the static so I
can focus and I have to have discipline and do them every day, to
see the light at the end of the tunnel and focus on each step
towards the bigger goal one at a time. Anyone can do this, and
anyone can succeed.

**I love seeing a beautiful kick-ass woman challenge the modern
misconception of witches - the *Handbook for Hot Witches* is my
kinda book - what is it about and what impact would you like
it to have on lady-kind?**
The *Handbook For Hot Witches* title comes from the same concept
that rappers use when they use the 'N' word to refer to
themselves. When you claim a word that was once derogatory, it
takes away the power of the people calling you the name.

Those who live in fear of the power of their own beauty and
un-conventionalism, feel threatened by the unique, intuitive,
creative, intelligent, strength of what the puritans call a 'Witch.'
What was the lesson of fascist, Nazi Germany? Just because
everyone is dong it, doesn't make it right.

I am all of these things and I see these magic and wonderful
qualities in other girls and all people. In this dominate-or-be-
dominated society, just by being born female we are supposed to
be 'the Bitch'. I deny this role, and I don't even notice it as an
option for me, or for anyone. This is why I choose liberty and life
and claim myself to be a Witch. My motto is 'Witches Not
Bitches'.

Genesis is a lie. Eve did not come from Adam's rib no more
than a Dad can give birth to his daughter. Lilith was created
before Eve to be equal with Adam and would rather have her
name slandered and live in 'Hell' than be Adam's bitch. The
snake goddess is a mermaid and is the oldest deity. She regen-

erates herself and like a snake has only been in hibernation this long cold winter of our discontent. The Dark Ages are over, and now in 2012, it is time for a renaissance. This is what Nostradamus and the Mayans spoke of. Native Americans know that our current society would run itself into the ground, and now that it has we can all start to live in sanity, but with the bonus of technology. All houses should be built to function like trees.

I am the embodiment of a magical creature, and the hard won facts and secrets I know to thrive and revolutionize a male dominated society on a dying planet I want to share with my witch sisters to make it all easier for everyone. When we live like faeries there will be no death, only life eternal.

My newest book, the *Handbook for Hot Witches* combines graphic novel with a 'how to' guide, add a dash of cook book and a fairy sprinkle of witch spell, wrap it all up with women's herstory and you have the *Handbook For Hot Witches*.

This is a girl's guide to the apocalypse. This book addresses the unique needs women have, and covers heavy issues like sustainable living once water, heat, and food have become scarce. It harkens back to an ancient time when women led as the herbalist healers, nurturers and disciplinarians of the community. But also looks to the future and gives advice on how to handle crisis in a time of global extremes, it addresses mood fluctuations, and how to handle inner turmoil.

Handbook For Hot Witches addresses our need for self-defense. It celebrates and acknowledges our inherent power of creativity, intuitiveness and every female role as a conduit to the spirit realm.

This guidebook is for girl scouts facing the realities of surviving in the jungle of today's political society with complex ecological implications. And gives them simple answers through philosophy, skill, crafts, and song to deal with these issues one step at a time through comics, fully illustrated step by step 'How

To's', in depth text with spot illustrations and a resource guide.

Most of women's history is blotted out from the pages of society. I profile 'witches' who stood out in the crowd, changed the world and fought for not just the rights of women, but for humanity and for justice. This book will help their legacy live on.

You're creatrix of the EZ Bake Coven too - can you tell us a little bit about that?

I first created it before Myspace/Facebook on my website so my friends and like-minded people could profile their amazing art and dolls. Now that all the social networking sites exist, I want to ultimately encourage real life interaction and group EZ Bake Coven meetings where people can encourage and support each other, and do rituals, etc. They will then post photos and comments from the EZ Bake Coven meeting in their city, on the community website, and share revelations /experiences with each other and make new contacts and friends. I think community, among women in particular, is important in today's society because so much about modern life and technology can be so isolating, and it's natural for women to want to hang out in family-like groups.

Here is an example of what I have in mind:

*E Z Bake Coven RITUAL STEPS for Hot Witches

1) Preparation: Dress fancy or wear and bring something special, this is a celebration! Observers are allowed who do not want to perform ritual. Nothing negative is allowed in this circle, only positive affirmations and support.

No one has to do anything they don't want to do; these are merely guidelines to help you connect to yourself, to your friends and to women from the past. This is not gender exclusive, guys and kids are allowed, but it is female-centric.

It's great to have goddess worshipers of all genders and ages. Mother nature gave birth to us all and will help anyone who knows how to ask.

2) Sit in a circle and introduce yourself, circle moves clockwise, feel free to OWN the term "Hot Witch" by inserting it in your name as a title, nick name, or what have you for example, Dame "Hot Witch" Darcy or "Hot Witch" Isabelle.

3) After you have said your name, celebrate the positive thing that you did or accomplished today. Even if you are having an otherwise bad day there is always something positive.

   It can range anywhere from "I taught a class to 25 kids, today we baked brownies and they turned out terrific" to "I passed the bar exam" to " I got rest today".

4) Friends in the circle congratulate, etc. and then the circle moves to the next person for introduction and what she wants to celebrate.

5) Everyone then gets a large piece of paper and a small piece of paper. On the large paper, write all your hopes dreams and desires. Take this home and post it on your bedroom door, or anywhere prominent where you can see it and remember it, as these things manifest in your life, check them off the list.

   On the other paper write one wish, this will be the one you are asking the goddess to help you manifest and with the power of yourself and your friends. Fold it, write your name on it, and put it in a box.

6) One person leads the ritual. Ritual profiles a witch from

history and something is read about her. Some research must be done before hand.

A really good resource I recommend is any of Judy Chicago's works. She published an amazing book called *The Dinner Party* which profiles thousands of women from the primordial goddess, to relatively modern America. Or look up goddesses and patron saints and then research Rituals that are done to honour them.

7) Perform the ritual. Chant, drink special things, the researcher of the ritual leads, or shows the others what the ritual is about. It doesn't have to be long or elaborate, just heart-felt.

8) When the ritual is done, sit in the circle and spin the bottle, the person the bottle lands on leads the next ritual. If she doesn't want to,spin again until it lands on some one willing.

9) Prayer for the dead (optional) "This prayer is for all the witches of the past who were burned and killed or fought for women's rights. We remember them and honour them now. May they rest in peace." Name a witch from history. Other coven members can add names of loved ones who have passed on in their own lives to this prayer. You can look up other prayers for the dead, Egyptian, Latin, Buddhist, anything you want and do it that way too.

10) Coven Meeting

   *When is the next ritual?

   *What will we celebrate? /Activities

   *Where is the next ritual?

*Questions comments

11) Have Fun! The goddess loves to see women enjoying themselves and that's what his is really all about!

12) Write about your coven experiences or your own thoughts/feelings on the EZ Bake coven forum, connect with other people and covens there. Post video blogs, get and give advice, etc.

13) We are magic!

What do you love most about being a woman?
That I am free to wear pretty glittery pink things, and the connection of friendship/sisterhood that women uniquely share is so fun. I survive on it and am so lucky and grateful for all my beautiful and talented witch-sisters and Faery-God Children and families and for the support of the great guys in my life.

What's your:
truth?
Seeking truth, liberty and life.
motto for life?
Frocks Not Jocks!
secret to success?
Follow through on every idea. Finish what you start. If you come to a brick wall where your skills won't allow you to get to the next step, admit when you can't do something and find some one to help, or learn how to do it yourself and keep going.
favourite book?
Here's some things I like:
Your Word is Your Wand by Florence Scovel Shinn
The Pagan Nun by Kate Horsley
Till We Have Faces by C.S. Lewis

Skinny Legs and All by Tom Robbins
Ethics Reincarnation and What It Means To Be Human by Joan Grant
Mama Gena's School of Womanly Arts by Regena Thomashauer
Ishmael by Daniel Quinn
The Power Of Now by Eckhart Tolle
Shambhala The Sacred Path of the Warrior by Chogyam Trungpa
Mermaid by Carolyn Turgeon
The Chalice and The Blade by Riane Eisler
The Dinner Party by Judy Chicago

I suggest anyone interested in learning about how things came to be, and who we are, read these heart-wrenching and enlightening tomes.
Poetry by:
Sappho
Shakesphere
Edgar Allan Poe
John Keats
Charles Baudilaire
Emily Dickinson
Christina Rosetti
And my most favorite and cherished Oscar Wilde
- most treasured item?
My" 85 year old French Boudoir Doll Isabelle (though she would kick me if she knew I called her an "Item")

This goddess-woman inspires me like no other, go look at her website, drool over her imagery, ask her to play in a band with you. www.damedarcy.com.

Now what?
High fives, g-friend, you have now discovered the keys to unlocking your SASSY superpowers. Your mission, should you choose to accept it, (and you absolutely should) is to now use

them to be as badass as possible, embrace your complete awesomeness and become mistress of your destiny. Y'know, the stuff of REAL super-hero-girls. Work your powers for good, live your best life, love hard, take risks, have AMAZING sex. Rocking your SASSY and shining so crazy bright in all you do is the most perfect permission slip to fellow lady-kind to do exactly the same. Now that you have SASSY superpowers, it would be simply rude and wrong to keep them a secret.

Tell every member of lady-kind you know that there's another way. They don't have to wear a li'l Miss Perfect mask, or compete, manipulate or hate on fellow members of the sisterhood. They don't need to use masculine qualities to trail blaze in the workplace or dance to the beat of someone else's life soundtrack. When you meet a woman who is not digging on her reflection in the mirror or is lost in a world of *should* and *could* scenarios, share the SASSY love.

It's the stuff that revolutions are made of and will literally save the world. It's what super-hero-girls do, and you are a super-hero-girl.

FACT.

UPDATE: Feb 2012 – Fairy tales DO exist

So, my book was all signed, sealed and ready to go to print, but I've managed to persuade the editor-types to hold the press so I could tell you my exciting news.

So, you know how Ohh-la-la land Paris has had a magickal starring role in my personal SASSY journey, don't you? And you also know how I manifested my beau, the hunk o' Viking love stuff, right? Well, last week the aforementioned hunk o' Viking love stuff whisked me off to Paris as a Christmas/ Valentines Day treat – how very ohh-la-la, non? We munched macaroons from *Laduree*, we walked hand-in-hand along the River Seine, ate crème brulee in *Café deux Moulin* ala *Amelie*, enjoyed the spectacle of the Moulin Rouge and wondered the streets o' Montmatre, channeling all the amazing creative types that had gone before us. Most importantly, we visited the Eiffel Tower, the tower of magick and sparkle, the place I go to when I want to make shit happen. We waited until dusk so we could watch the sunset over the delicious city of Par-ee, and right there, at the top of my most favourite, magickal spot in the whole wide world, my hunk o' Viking love stuff, got down on one knee and asked me to marry him.

It was the stuff o' my pink-tinted dreams.

I made eye-water. A lot. It was the sweetest, most delicious moment of my entire life. What's that? What did I say? *Oui*, of course. Have you seen him? He's HAWT. And do you know what? While I know I'm crazy lucky to have met, and now be engaged to, a man like him, he's getting the real deal too. I'm a super SASSY minx who knows how awesome she is, who laughs a little too loud, who is super-emo (especially when watching chick flicks), has an unhealthy obsession for chocolate, messes up on a regular basis and can make crazy-good Pad Thai.

It's true, fairy tales DO exist, but the deal is, and it's a pretty big deal btw, it's up to YOU to write them.

Yep, to add *real* magick and sparkle to your life, you have to call the shots, take the reigns and rule *your* world.

Forget the days when fairy tales were all about the perfect happy ending, anyone with an ounce o' SASSY knows that the most bliss-kissed, fun-filled life is lived RIGHT NOW. Be in the moment; connect to source/universe/goddess/spiritual homies and open your heart as wide as it will go. Dream big dreams, face your fears, overcome challenges, take responsibility for your actions and show up, every single day, to make the good stuff happen.

How your story develops is completely up to you. What you fill the pages of your memoir with is completely your choice. You are the author of your book, director of your movie, star of your show – so take charge and give yourself something to smile about

– I dare you.

Oh and remember, see the beauty and glitter-filled potential in absolutely everything, it's the law. According to me.

SASSY resources

I heart books. Here are some of my favourites that I've read whilst on my own SASSY road trip – borrow them, buy them, most importantly read them.

Books are the best.

SELF HELP-Y GOODNESS
Crazy Sexy Diet – Kris Carr`
The Way of the Happy Woman – Sara Avant Stover
Raw Emotions – Angela Stokes
Eating in the Light – Doreen Virtue
Losing your Pounds of Pain – Doreen Virtue
I could do anything if only I knew what it was – Barbara Sher
Authentic Woman – Leslie and Susannah Kenton
The Body Sacred – Dianne Sylvan
The Artist's Way – Julia Cameron
Live like a Hot Chick – Jodi Lipper & Cerina Vincent

VINTAGE/FASHION-Y FABULOUSNESS
Pretty Things – Liz Goldman
Cherry Bomb – Carrie Borzillo Vreena
Style Me Vintage – Katie Reynolds
Tease – Immodesty Blaize
Ambition – Immodesty Blaize
The Burlesque Handbook – Jo Boobs Weldon
The Modern Girl's Guide To Fabulousness – Bethanie Lunn

OHH LA LA
Anything by Anais Nin – I HEART all her books - read them, love them.
Corsets: A Modern Guide – Velda Lauder
Tropic of Cancer – Henry Miller

Becoming Orgasmic – Julia R. Heiman

KICK-ASSNESS
The Power of Influence – Sarah Prout
Spiritual Business – Kate Forster
The Right Brain Business Plan – Jennifer Lee
Rich Dad's Conspiracy of the Rich – the 8 new rules of money – Robert T Kiyosaki
Heroines: The bold, the bad and the beautiful – Jessica Ruston
Business as Unusual: My Entrepreneurial Journey – Anita Roddick
Absolutely Now – Lynne Franks
Lessons of a Lipstick Queen – Poppy King

SPIRITUAL YUMMYNESS
The Red Book – Sara Beak
73 Lessons Every Goddess Must Know – Goddess Leonie Dawson
How to be a Spiritual Goddess: Bring a Little Cosmic Magic into Your Life – Stephanie Brookes
The Red Tent – Anita Diamant
The Forty Rules of Love – Elif Shafak
Women, Food & God – Geneen Roth
The goddess guide to chakra vitality – Anita Ryan
The Journey – Brandon Bays
All Women are Psychics – Diane Stein
Goddesses in Everywoman – Jean Shinoda Bolen
Everyday Enlightenment – how to be a spiritual warrior at the kitchen sink – Venerable Yeshe Chodron
Spiritual Growth – being your higher self – Sanaya Roman
Going Within – A guide for inner transformation – Shirley Maclaine
Creative Visualisation – Shakti Gawain
White Magic – Lucy Cavendish

Awaken your Goddess – Liz Simpson

Sacred & Naked – Ruth Ostrow

The High Heeled Guide to Enlightenment – Alice Grist

The High Heeled Guide to Spiritual Living – Alice Grist

About the author-girl

I'm Lisa Clark, creatrix of SASSYology – the awesomeness that occurs when women discover, align and combine their SASSY super-powers – yee-hah. I live it, study it, teach it, write about it. I'm a tattoo-splashed, burlesque-lovin', belly-dancin', 1940s stylin' rockabilly princess who writes make-life-better words for love AND money. I'm agony aunt for teen magazine *Mizz*. I drink a LOT of green tea. I kiss my beau. I shake my tail feather. I believe in love. I am a bravado-boostin' self-esteem coach for go-for-it girls and I LOVE it. I'm rarely seen without hot pink lipstick and I'm crazy-passionate about cheerleading ladykind to become the mistress of their destiny.

Find out more about me, my work and my ability to accessorise at: **www.sassyology.com**

Please send me love notes at: **lisa@sassyology.com**

**SASSY
BOOKS**

Hip, real and raw, SASSY books share authentic truths, spiritual insights and entrepreneurial witchcraft with women who want to kick ass in life and y'know...start revolutions.